SCHOLASTIC

Reading & Math

This book belongs to

_____

Cover design by Sequel Creative
Cover art by Patrick Girouard
Interior illustrations by Janet Armbrust, Jane Dippold, Rusty Fletcher,
Sherry Neidigh, Karen Sevaly, and Carol Tiernon.

ISBN 0-439-78598-7

16 17 18 19 20   08   20 19 18 17 16

Dear Parents,

The power to succeed is in every child! The question is: How can you help your child achieve this success and become an independent, lifelong learner?

You have already taken the first step! *Reading & Math* is the perfect way to support the learning your child needs to be successful in school.

Research shows that independent practice helps children gain mastery of essential skills. This book includes carefully selected, teacher-tested activities that give preschool children exactly the practice they need. Topics covered include:

- Letter Recognition
- Sight Words
- Handwriting
- Number Recognition
- Counting
- Early Concepts

You'll also find assessments to help you keep track of your child's progress—and provide important practice with standardized test formats.

Let's get started! Your involvement will make this a valuable educational experience and will support and enhance your child's learning.

Enjoy!

Hindie

Hindie Weissman
Educational Consultant,
27+ years teaching experience

PRE K Learn and Succeed

Welcome to *Reading & Math!*

PreK is a critical stepping stone on the road to learning success! This workbook has been carefully designed to help ensure your child has the tools he or she needs to soar in school. On the 300-plus pages that follow, you'll find plenty of practice in each of these must-know curriculum areas:

ALPHABET	READING READINESS	WORD BUILDING	EARLY CONCEPTS
• Identifying Letters • Sequencing Letters • Writing Letters	• Classifying Objects • Sequencing Stories • Recognizing Similarities and Differences	• Mastering Sight Words • Mastering Color Words • Mastering Science and Social Studies Words	• Identifying Opposites • Comparing Sizes • Sorting and Classifying
NUMBERS	MATH CONCEPTS	FOLLOWING DIRECTIONS	THINKING SKILLS
• Identifying Numbers • Counting • Writing Numbers	• Identifying Shapes • Understanding Patterns • Using Pictures to Solve Problems	• Building Listening Skills • Performing Steps in Sequence • Taking Bubble Tests	• Identifying Sets • Recognizing Relationships • Simple Reasoning

Helping your child build essential skills is easy!

These teacher-approved activities have been specially developed to make learning both accessible and enjoyable. On each page, you'll find:

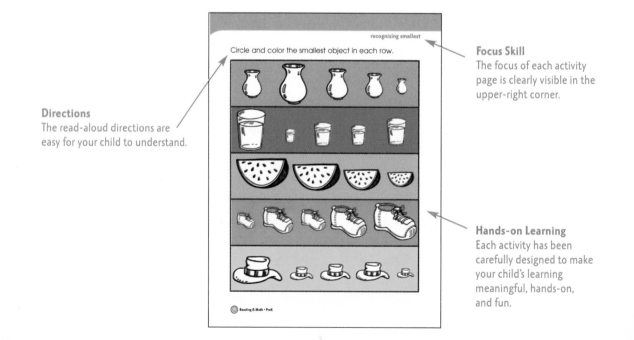

Directions
The read-aloud directions are easy for your child to understand.

Focus Skill
The focus of each activity page is clearly visible in the upper-right corner.

Hands-on Learning
Each activity has been carefully designed to make your child's learning meaningful, hands-on, and fun.

Scholastic

with Reading & Math!

These great extras are guaranteed to make learning extra engaging!

Reading & Math is loaded with lots of motivating, special components including:

SPECIAL ACTIVITIES TO GET READY FOR KINDERGARTEN ▶

Give your child a head start in kindergarten with this BONUS assortment of get-ready activities.

◀ CONNECTION TO ONLINE LEARNING

Boost computer literacy with this special link to a treasury of skill-building online activities at www.scholastic.com/success.

MOTIVATING STICKERS ▶

Mark the milestones of your child's learning path with these bright, kid-pleasing stickers.

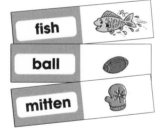

◀ INSTANT FLASH CARDS

Promote reading fluency with these fun, colorful flash cards.

REWARD CERTIFICATE ▶

Celebrate your child's leap in learning with this colorful, pull-out completion certificate.

◀ LIST OF THE BEST BOOKS FOR YOUNG LEARNERS

Reinforce key concepts and build a love of reading with this great list of learning-rich books selected by top educators. See page 12.

QUICK ASSESSMENT TESTS ▶

Make sure your child *really* masters each must-know skill with the instant assessment tests that conclude each section.

Table of Contents

Scholastic

Scholastic

MATHEMATICS

Scholastic

Scholastic

Tips for Success

Here are some tips to help your child get the most out of this workbook:

- Provide a quiet, comfortable place for your child to work.

- Make sure your child understands the directions.

- Encourage your child to use colorful pencils and markers to make learning fun.

- Check completed work as soon as possible and review corrected work with your child.

- Pay attention to areas where your child is having difficulty. Spend extra time to help him or her master those skills.

- Provide a special area at home where your child's work can be displayed.

- Be positive and encouraging. Praise your child for his or her efforts and good work.

Scholastic

Read with Your Child

Reading to your child and having him or her read to you is an extremely effective way of supporting your child's learning. When you read with him or her, make sure your child is actively participating. Here are five ways to support your child's reading:

1. Let your child choose the book.

2. Look at the cover of the book and ask your child what he or she thinks the story will be about.

3. As you read the book, locate a good stopping point and ask your child to predict what will happen next. Then read to confirm the prediction or correct it.

4. Discuss the characters in the story: Are they kind? good? bad? clever? Are they like characters in another book?

5. When you finish the story, have your child retell it.

Scholastic

Read with Your Child

Looking for a great book to read to your child? Here are some top teacher picks:

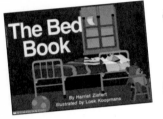

- *Alphabet Soup: A Feast of Letters* by Scott Gustafson (Greenwich Workshop Press, 1996).

- *The Bed Book* by Harriet Ziefert (Scholastic, 1981).

- *Dr. Seuss's ABC, I Can Read It All By Myself Beginner Book* by Dr. Seuss (Random House Books for Young Readers, 1996).

- *The House That Jack Built* by Elizabeth Falconer (LC Publishing, 1985).

- *Lunch* by Denise Fleming (Henry Holt, 1992).

- *Miss Bindergarten Gets Ready for Kindergarten* by Joseph Slate (Penguin Putnam, 2001).

- *An Octopus Followed Me Home* by Dan Yaccarino (Viking, 1997)

- *Picnic* by Emily McCully (Harper Row, 1984).

- *School Bus* by Donald Crews (Viking Penguin, 1984).

- *There's a Zoo in Room 22* by Judy Sierra (Harcourt, 2000).

The Alphabet/Handwriting

"I can write my ABC's!" is a wonderful thing for a parent to hear a child say. Recognizing letters, writing them, and knowing the sounds they make are all essential skills in learning to read and write. The pages in this section give kids lots of practice in all of these skills.

What to Do

On the letter-writing practice pages, have your child use a pencil to trace, and then write, the letter. When finished, invite him or her to circle their "best letter" on each page.

Once your child completes this section, encourage him or her to review the word and picture pages for each letter. Reviewing these words regularly will help your child develop reading and vocabulary skills during the year!

Keep On Going!

• Challenge your child to find certain letters in the world around them: on signs, pieces of mail, license plates, and so on.

• Focus on your child's name. The letters in a child's name are often the ones he or she recognizes and writes first. Build confidence by having your child sign his or her art work and notes and letters to friends and family.

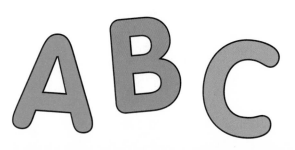

Identify and write the letters.
Color the picture.

Uppercase A

Lowercase a

Say the words. Color the pictures.

apple	
angel	
alligator	
anchor	

Identify and write the letters.
Color the picture.

Uppercase B

Lowercase b

Scholastic

Say the words. Color the pictures.

book

boots

bell

bicycle

Identify and write the letters.
Color the picture.

Uppercase C

C C C C C C C

Lowercase c

c c c c c c

Say the words. Color the pictures.

car	
cup	
cow	
candle	

Identify and write the letters.
Color the picture.

Uppercase D

Lowercase d

Scholastic

Say the words. Color the pictures.

duck	
dog	
door	
dinosaur	

Identify and write the letters.
Color the picture.

Uppercase E

Lowercase e

Say the words. Color the pictures.

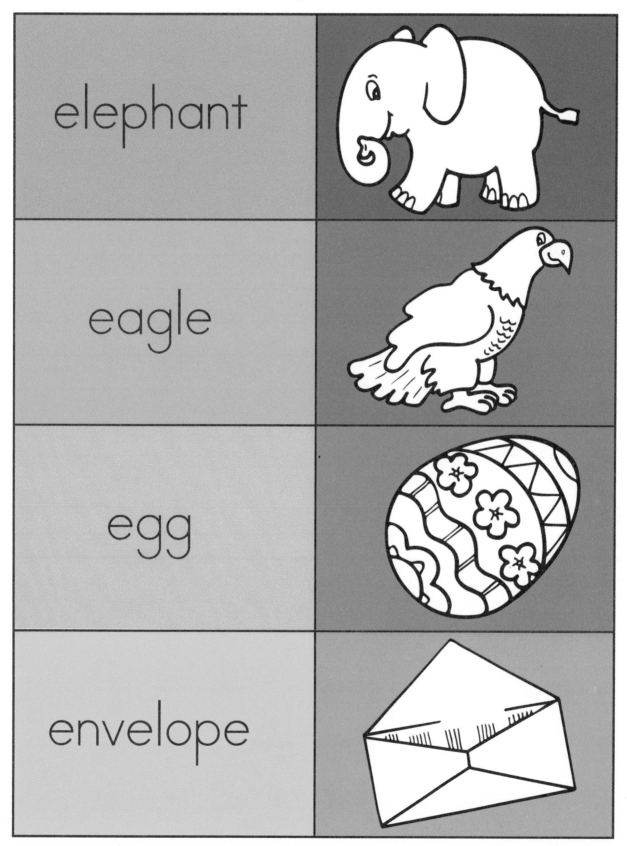

elephant	
eagle	
egg	
envelope	

Scholastic

Identify and write the letters.
Color the picture.

Uppercase F

Lowercase f

Say the words. Color the pictures.

fox	
fork	
fish	
fan	

Scholastic

Identify and write the letters.
Color the picture.

Uppercase G

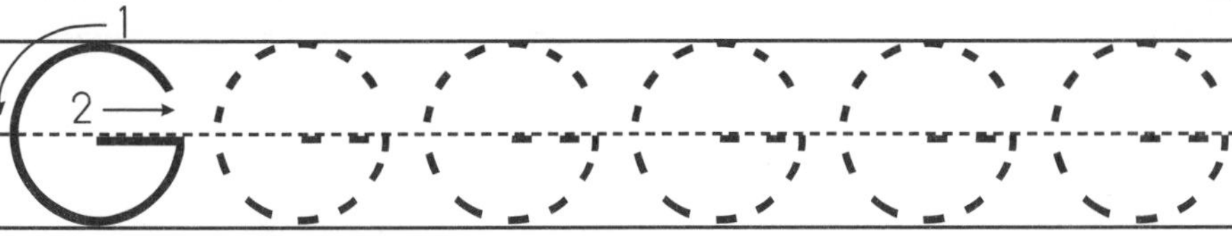

G G G G G G

Lowercase g

g g g g g g

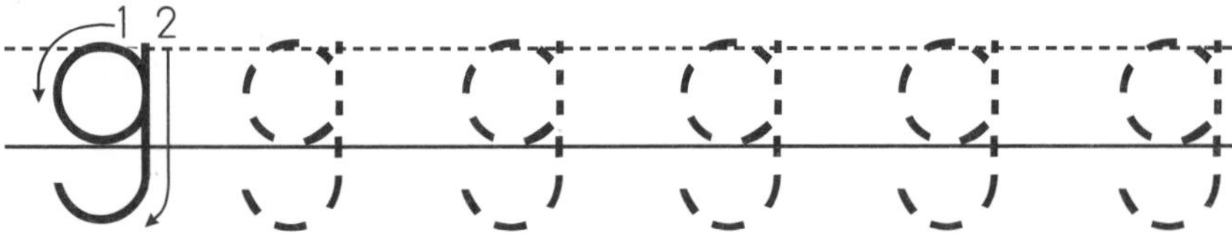

Scholastic

Say the words. Color the pictures.

goat

guitar

ghost

gate

Identify and write the letters.
Color the picture.

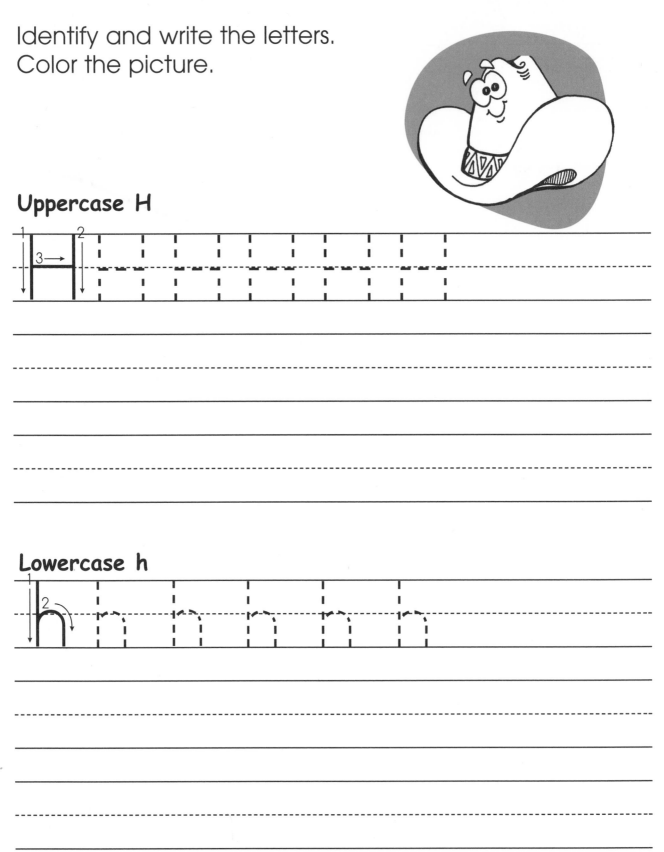

Uppercase H

Lowercase h

Scholastic

Say the words. Color the pictures.

horn	
helicopter	
horse	
hammer	

Draw lines to connect the matching uppercase and lowercase letters.

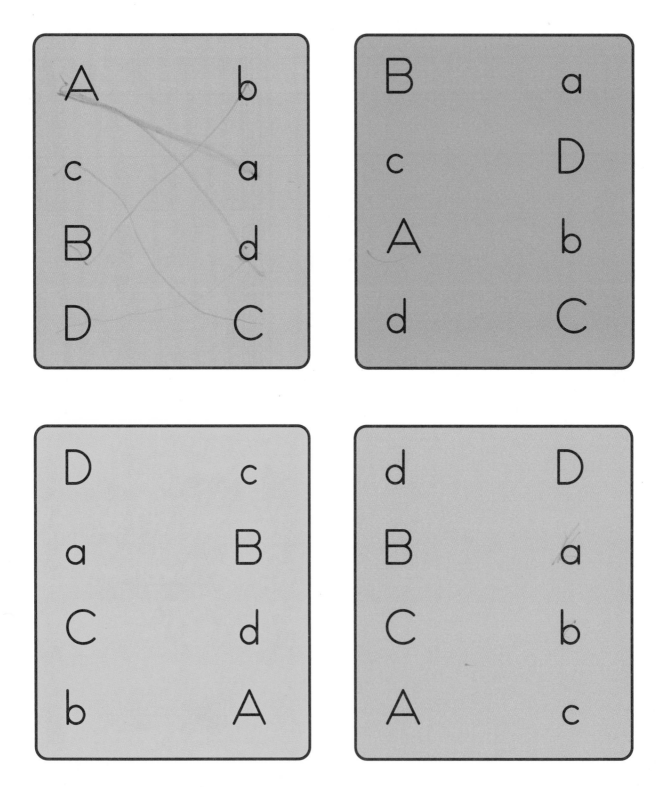

A	b
c	a
B	d
D	C

B	a
c	D
A	b
d	C

D	c
a	B
C	d
b	A

d	D
B	a
C	b
A	c

Draw lines to connect the matching uppercase and lowercase letters.

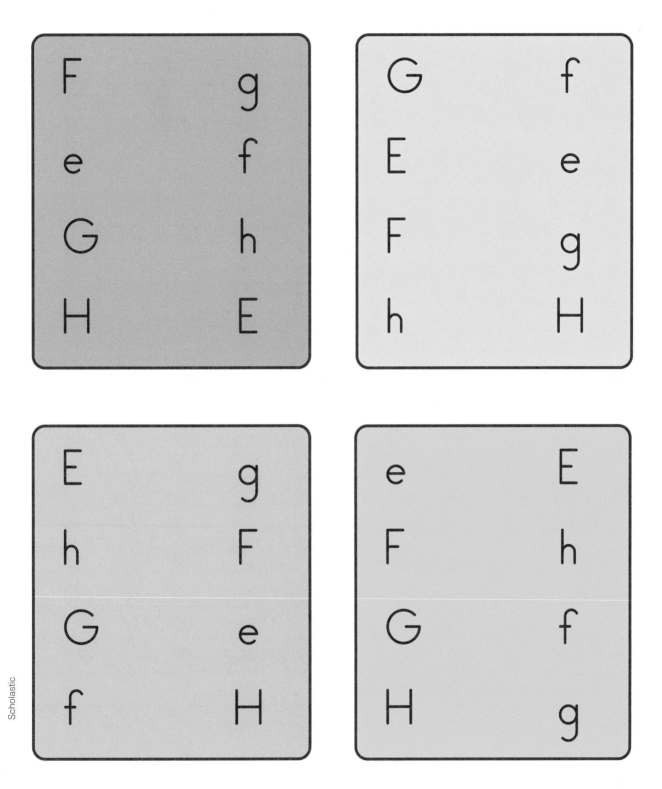

Identify and write the letters.
Color the picture.

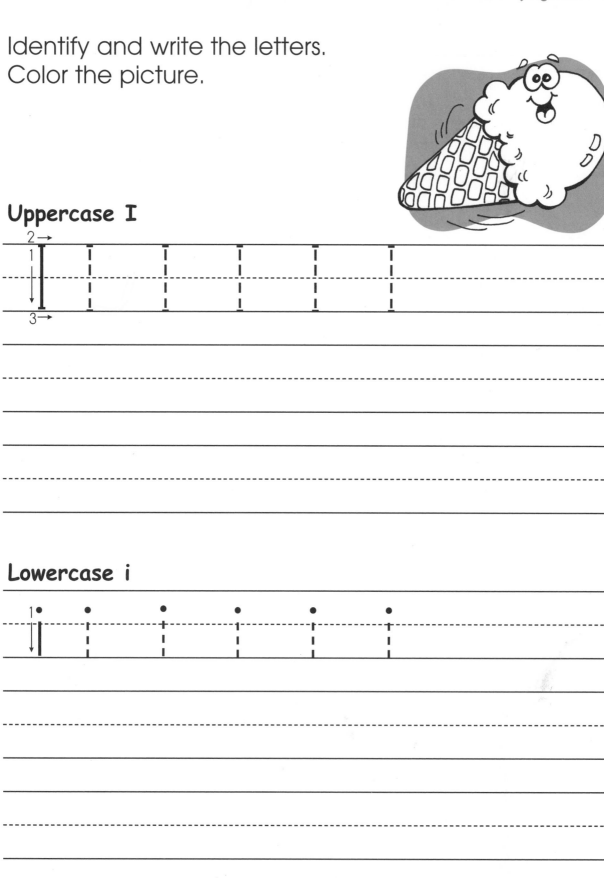

Uppercase I

Lowercase i

Say the words. Color the pictures.

igloo

insect

ice cream

iron

Identify and write the letters.
Color the picture.

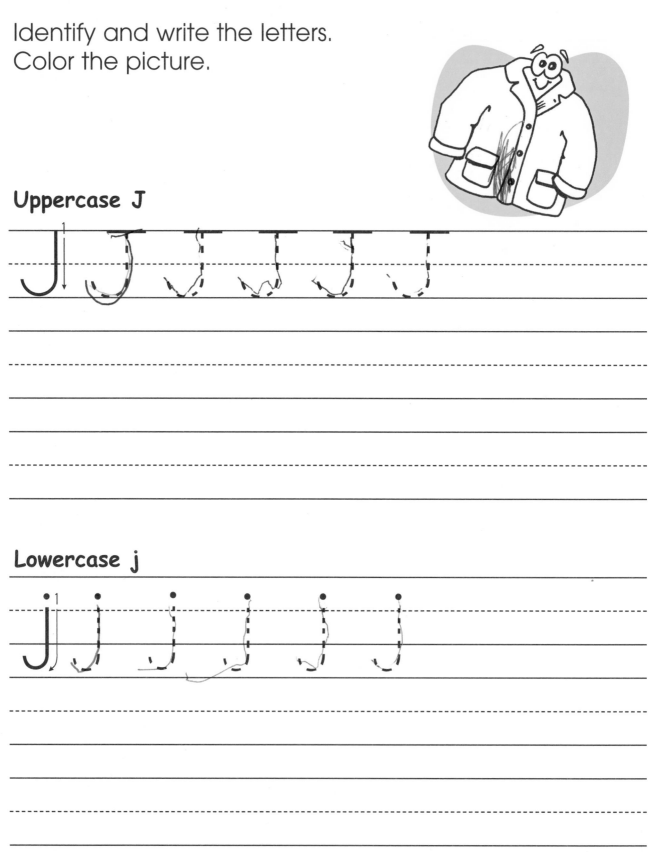

Uppercase J

Lowercase j

Say the words. Color the pictures.

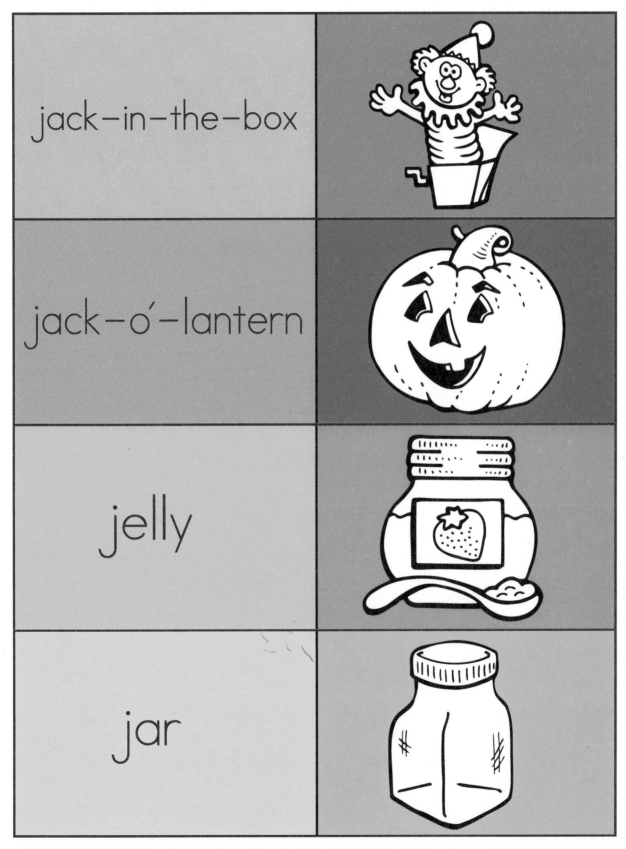

jack-in-the-box	
jack-o'-lantern	
jelly	
jar	

Identify and write the letters.
Color the picture.

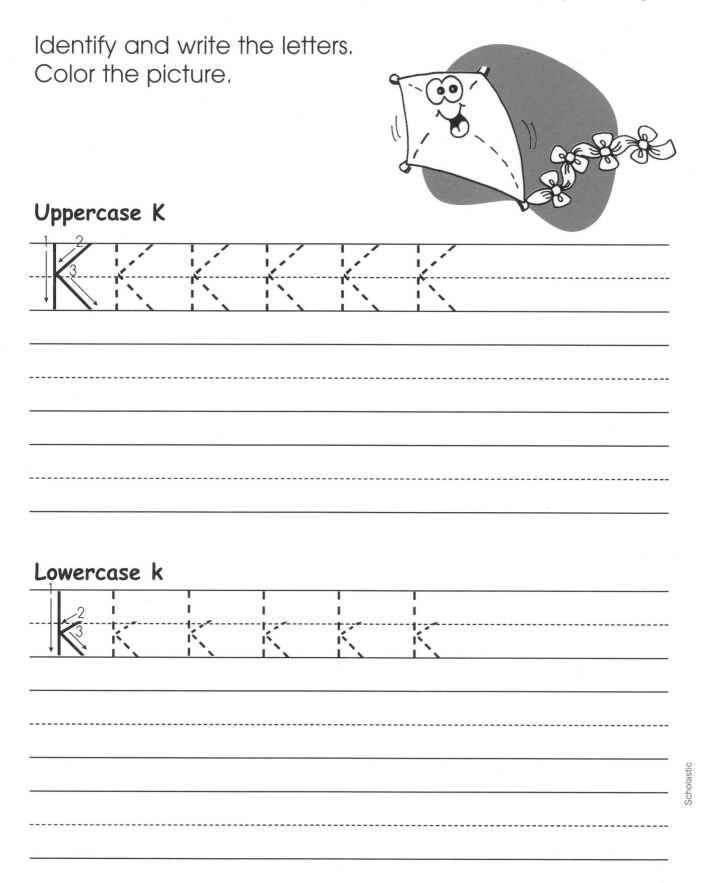

Uppercase K

Lowercase k

Say the words. Color the pictures.

kangaroo	
keys	
king	
kite	

Scholastic

Identify and write the letters.
Color the picture.

Uppercase L

Lowercase l

Say the words. Color the pictures.

lion	
ladder	
light bulb	
lamb	

Identify and write the letters.
Color the picture.

Uppercase M

Lowercase m

Say the words. Color the pictures.

monkey	
mitten	
moon	
mouse	

Identify and write the letters.
Color the picture.

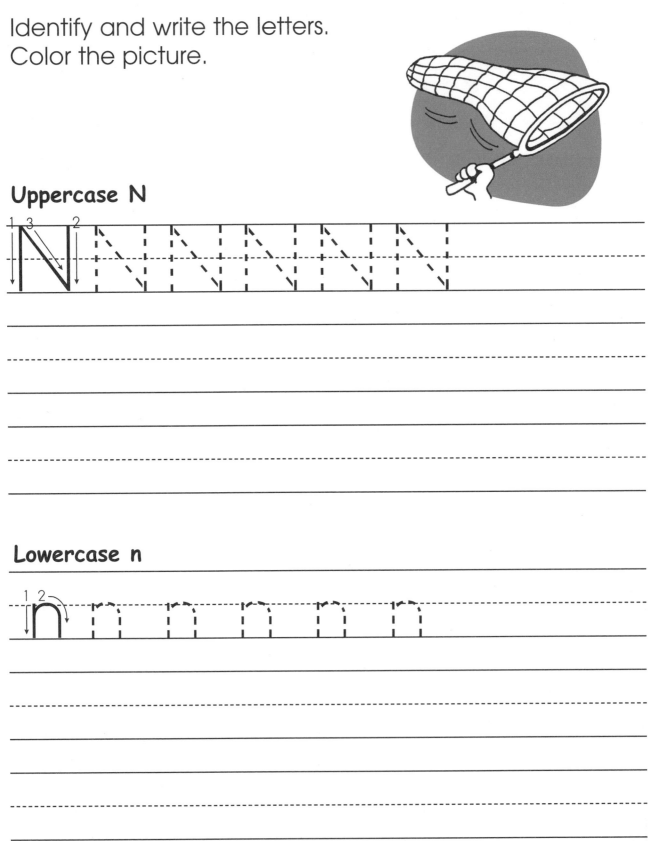

Uppercase N

Lowercase n

Scholastic

Say the words. Color the pictures.

nuts

needle

newspaper

nest

Identify and write the letters.
Color the picture.

Uppercase O

Lowercase o

Scholastic

Say the words. Color the pictures.

owl

octopus

orange

ostrich

Identify and write the letters.
Color the picture.

Uppercase P

Lowercase p

Say the words. Color the pictures.

pencil	
pear	
parachute	
piano	

Draw lines to connect the matching uppercase and lowercase letters.

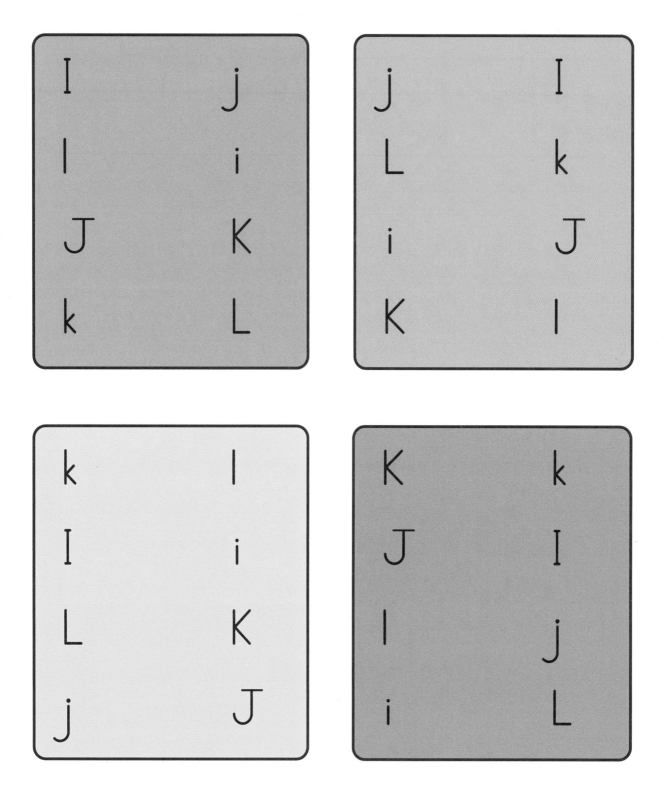

Draw lines to connect the matching uppercase and lowercase letters.

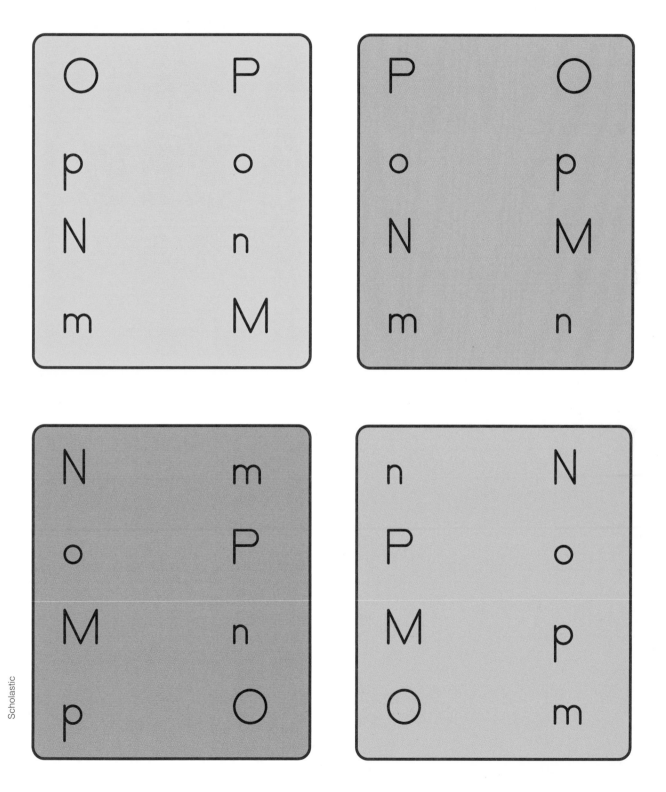

O	P
p	o
N	n
m	M

P	O
o	p
N	M
m	n

N	m
o	P
M	n
p	O

n	N
P	o
M	p
O	m

Scholastic

Identify and write the letters.
Color the picture.

Uppercase Q

Lowercase q

Scholastic

Say the words. Color the pictures.

quail	
queen	
quilt	
question mark	

Identify and write the letters.
Color the picture.

Uppercase R

Lowercase r

Say the words. Color the pictures.

rainbow	
rabbit	
rake	
rocket	

Identify and write the letters.
Color the picture.

Uppercase S

S S S S S S

Lowercase s

s s s s s s

Say the words. Color the pictures.

saw

sun

soap

sink

Identify and write the letters.
Color the picture.

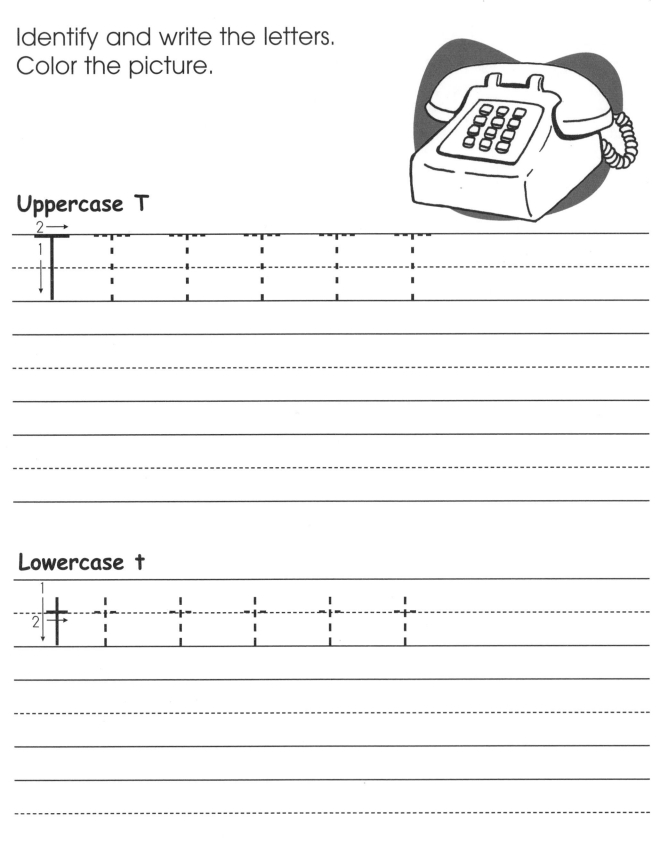

Uppercase T

Lowercase t

Scholastic

Say the words. Color the pictures.

top	
toothbrush	
turtle	
tree	

Scholastic

Identify and write the letters.
Color the picture.

Uppercase U

U U U U U U

Lowercase u

u u u u u u

Say the words. Color the pictures.

umbrella	
unicorn	
United States	
unicycle	

Identify and write the letters.
Color the picture.

Be Mine!

Uppercase V

Lowercase v

Say the words. Color the pictures.

vest	
violin	
valentine	
volcano	

Identify and write the letters.
Color the picture.

Uppercase W

Lowercase w

Reading & Math • PreK

Say the words. Color the pictures.

watermelon	
whale	
watch	
wagon	

Identify and write the letters.
Color the picture.

Uppercase X Y Z

Lowercase x y z

Scholastic

Say the words. Color the pictures.

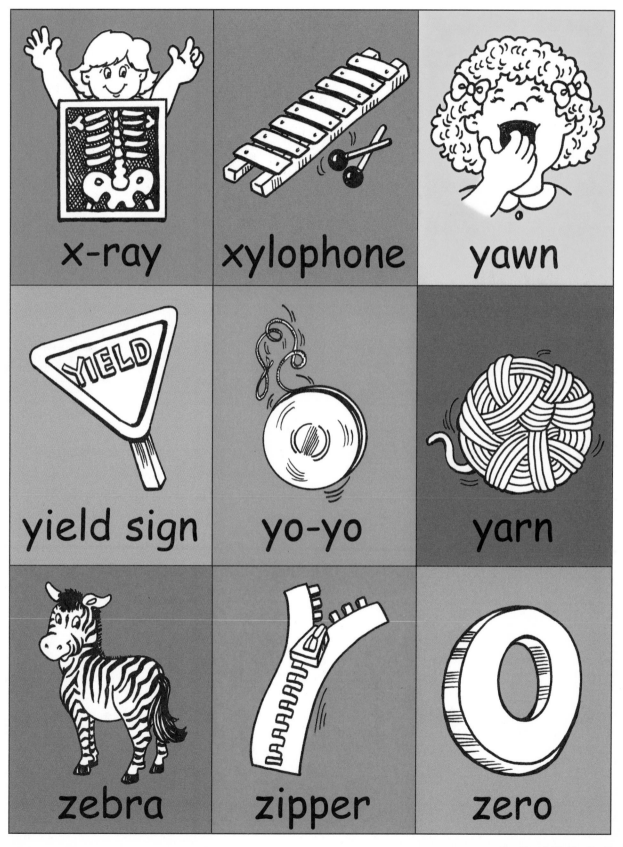

x-ray

xylophone

yawn

yield sign

yo-yo

yarn

zebra

zipper

zero

Scholastic

Draw lines to connect the matching uppercase and lowercase letters.

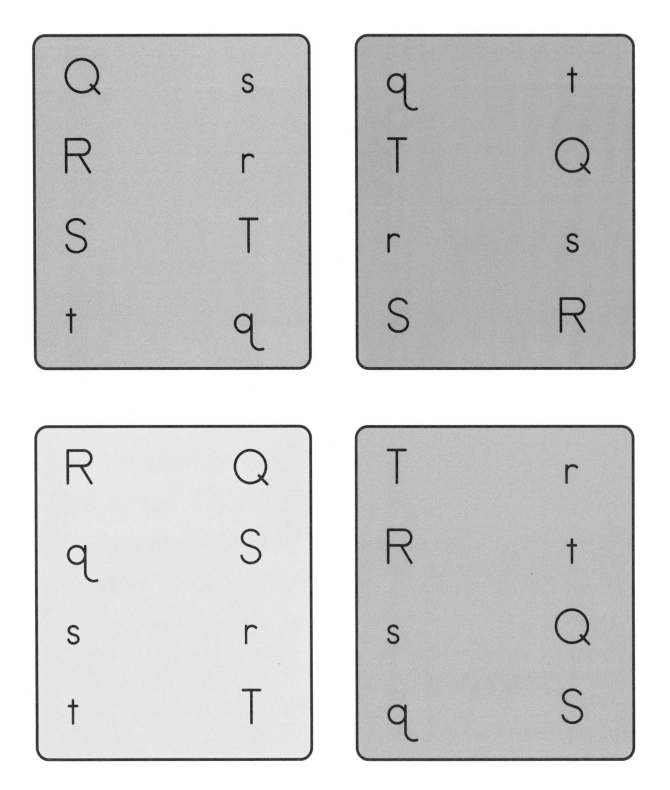

Draw lines to connect the matching uppercase and lowercase letters.

W	V
v	w
X	U
u	x

X	Y
y	x
Z	W
w	z

V	y
u	Z
Y	v
z	U

v	V
u	w
Y	y
W	U

Scholastic

Connect the dots from **A** to **Z**.

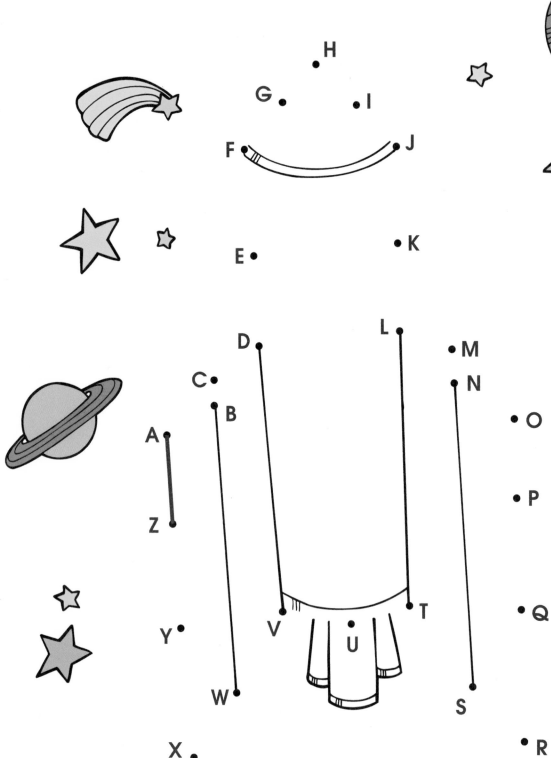

Scholastic

Alphabet Practice Test

Choose the letter that comes next. Color in the bubble next to that letter.

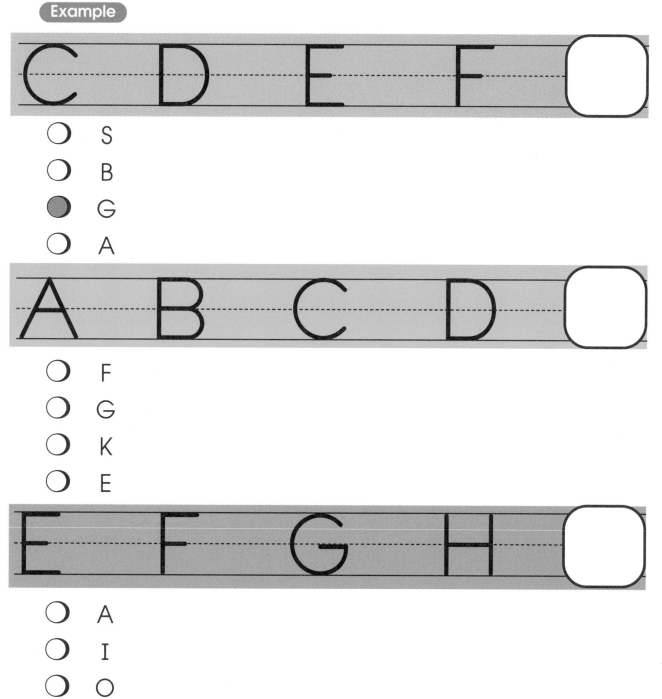

Example

C D E F ⬜

- ◯ S
- ◯ B
- ⬤ G
- ◯ A

A B C D ⬜

- ◯ F
- ◯ G
- ◯ K
- ◯ E

E F G H ⬜

- ◯ A
- ◯ I
- ◯ O
- ◯ P

Scholastic

Alphabet Practice Test

Choose the letter that comes next. Color in the bubble next to that letter.

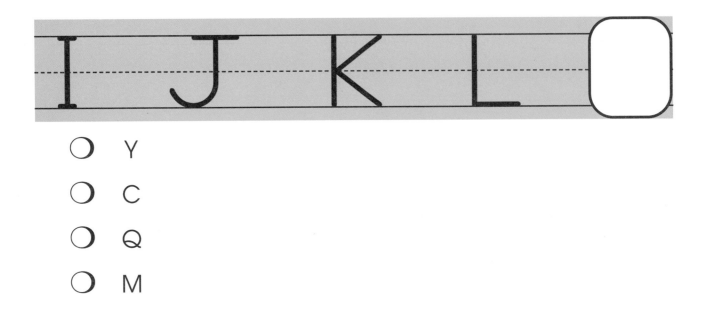

- ◯ Y
- ◯ C
- ◯ Q
- ◯ M

- ◯ N
- ◯ Q
- ◯ L
- ◯ M

Scholastic

Alphabet Practice Test

Choose the letter that comes next. Color in the bubble next to that letter.

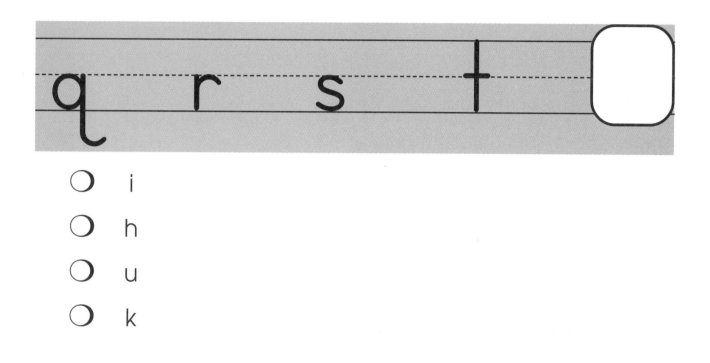

- ○ i
- ○ h
- ○ u
- ○ k

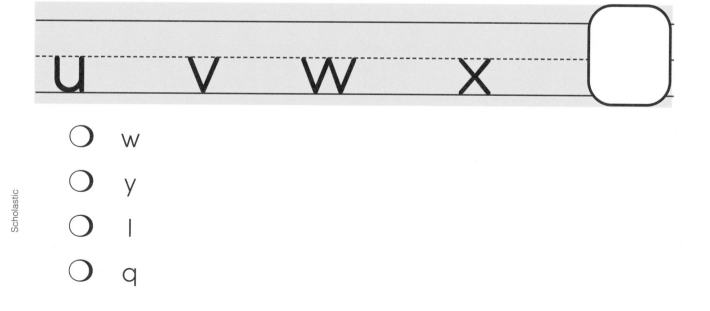

- ○ w
- ○ y
- ○ l
- ○ q

Scholastic

Alphabet Practice Test

Choose the letter that comes next.
Color in the bubble next to that letter.

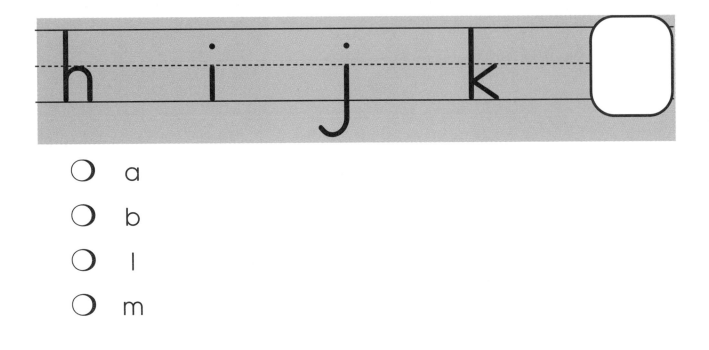

h i j k

- ○ a
- ○ b
- ○ l
- ○ m

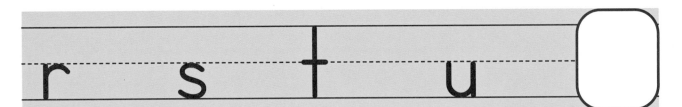

r s t u

- ○ w
- ○ h
- ○ j
- ○ v

Scholastic

Following Directions

Following directions is an essential skill in the classroom, in test taking and, of course, in life! Being able to follow a sequence of steps, whether written or spoken, is important for school success.

What to Do

These activities provide simple directions that children can follow to complete a fun activity. Read the directions to your child. Then have him or her complete the activity. Help your child check the work when finished.

Keep On Going!

• When performing everyday tasks, such as making a sandwich or opening a door with keys, invite your child to describe the procedure in simple steps using words like *first, next, then,* and so on. (For instance, "First you take out the keys, next you put them in the keyhole, then you turn them and the door opens.")

• Praise your child whenever he or she follows your verbal directions and point out that listening carefully is great practice for school.

What yummy treat is Lisa eating?

① **Draw** a line connecting the numbers from 1 to 10.

② **Draw** a line from the circle to Lisa's hand.

③ **Color** the treat red.

Scholastic

Help put things away in the classroom.

(1) **Look** at the classroom.

(2) **Draw** lines to show where each thing goes.

Scholastic

Cars come in different colors.

(1) **Color** three cars red.

(2) **Color** two cars blue.

○

(3) **Draw** a circle around the car carrying a dog.

Scholastic

Can you find the numbers?

(1) **Draw** a circle around each number.

(2) **Color** the picture.

Scholastic

One home in each row is not like the others.

(1) **Look** at the homes.

(2) **Draw** a circle around the home in each row

that does not match the others.

Scholastic

Everyone must follow rules to stay safe.

(1) **Look** at the pictures.

(2) **Draw** a circle around the child in each row

who is being safe.

Scholastic

Following Directions Practice Test

Read the directions to your child.

1. Find the spider. Hint: a spider has eight legs. Fill in the bubble next to that spider.

○ **A**

○ **B**

○ **C**

○ **D**

2. Find the ladybug. Hint: she has dots on her back. Fill in the bubble next to the ladybug.

○ **F**

○ **G**

○ **H**

○ **J**

Scholastic

Following Directions Practice Test

Read the directions to your child.

3. Fill in the bubble next to clothing for a cold day.

○ **A**

○ **B**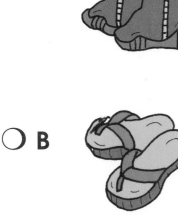

○ **C**

○ **D**

4. Fill in the bubble next to clothing for a hot day.

○ **F**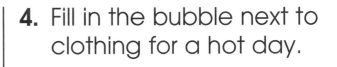

○ **G**

○ **H**

○ **J**

Scholastic

Following Directions Practice Test

Read the directions to your child.

5. Fill in the bubble next to the picture that shows what you wear on your head.

○ **A**

○ **B**

○ **C**

○ **D**

6. Fill in the bubble next to the picture that shows what you wear on your hands.

○ **F**

○ **G**

○ **H**

○ **J**

Scholastic

Following Directions Practice Test

Read the directions to your child.

7. Fill in the bubble next to the picture that shows a teacher at the chalkboard.

○ A

○ B

○ C

○ D

8. Fill in the bubble next to the house that is different.

○ F

○ G

○ H

○ J

Basic Concepts

Concepts such as size, direction, and location are important across the entire school curriculum. These pages give your child lots of practice with these basic concepts.

What to Do

Read the directions on each page to your child. When finished, help your child check his or her work. Offer lots of praise for doing such a great job!

Keep On Going!

Weave the vocabulary of these concepts into everyday conversations. For instance, if you are looking at shells on the beach with your child, you might say, "Can you find the smallest shell?" When giving your child tasks to do at home, use positional words, such as "Please put the book *below* the shelf of toys."

Circle and color the largest object in each row.

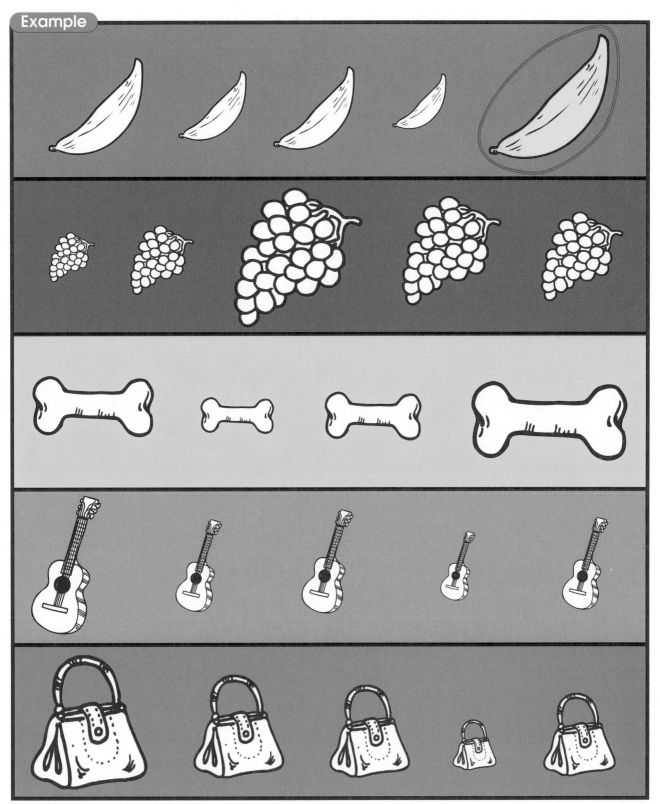

Example

Circle and color the largest object in each row.

Scholastic

Circle and color the smallest object in each box.

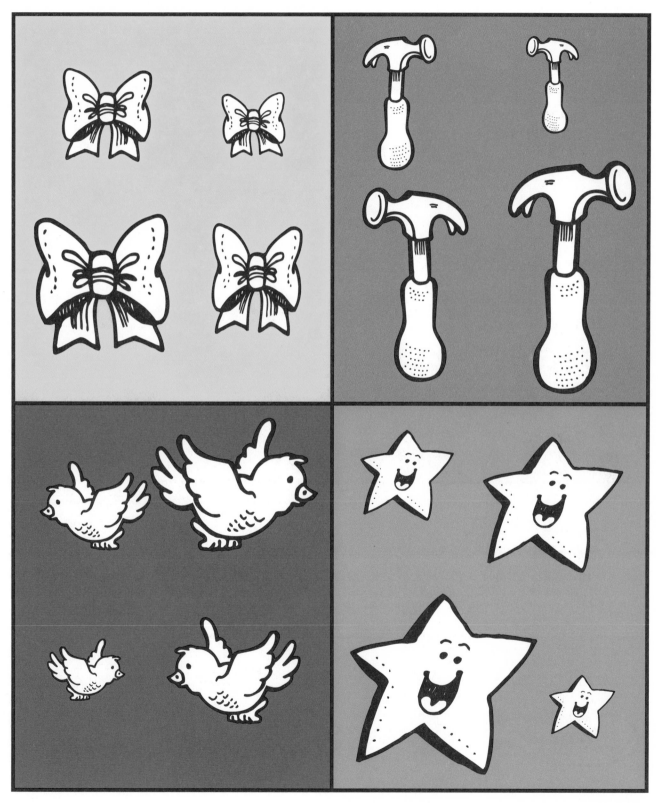

Circle and color the smallest object in each row.

Color all of the large apples red.

Color all of the small apples green.

Color all of the large cakes yellow.

Color all of the small cakes brown.

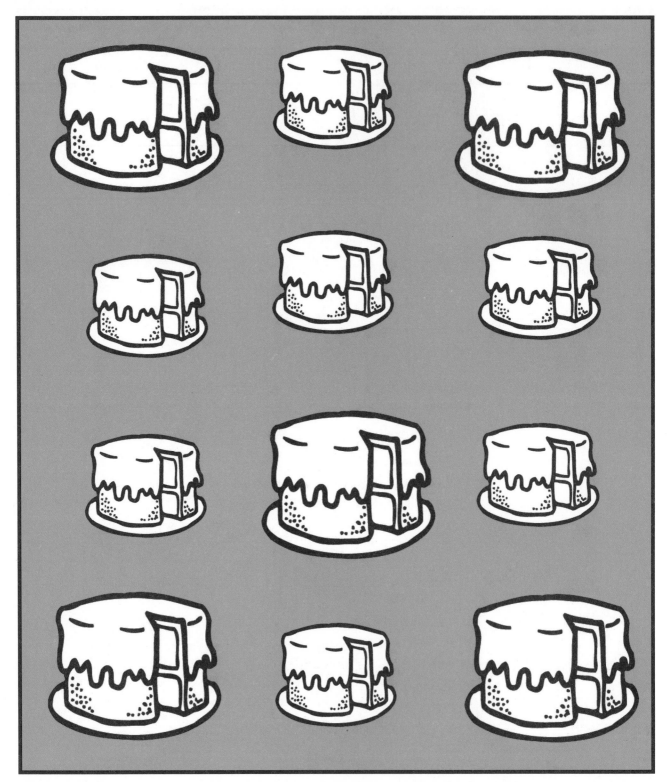

Circle and color the longest object in each box.

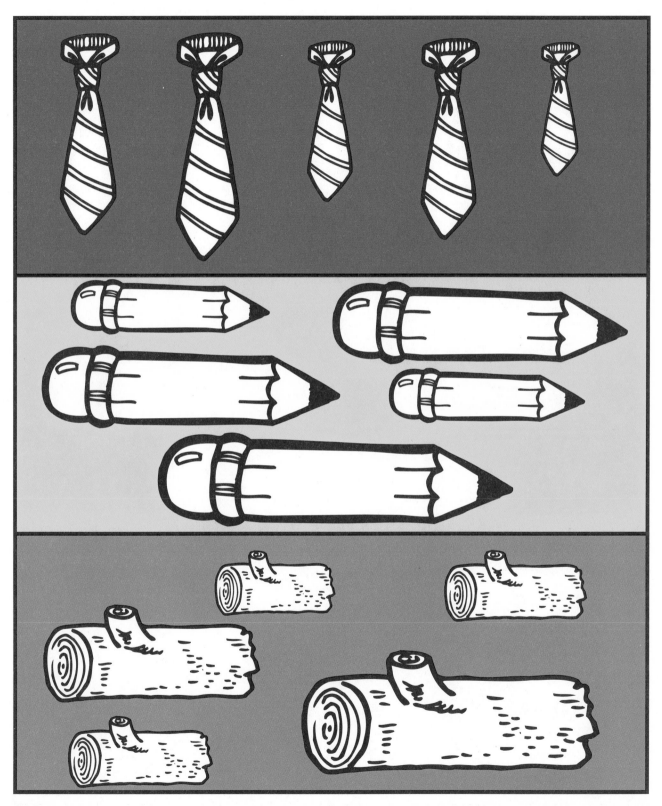

Color the long toothbrushes blue.

Color the short toothbrushes green.

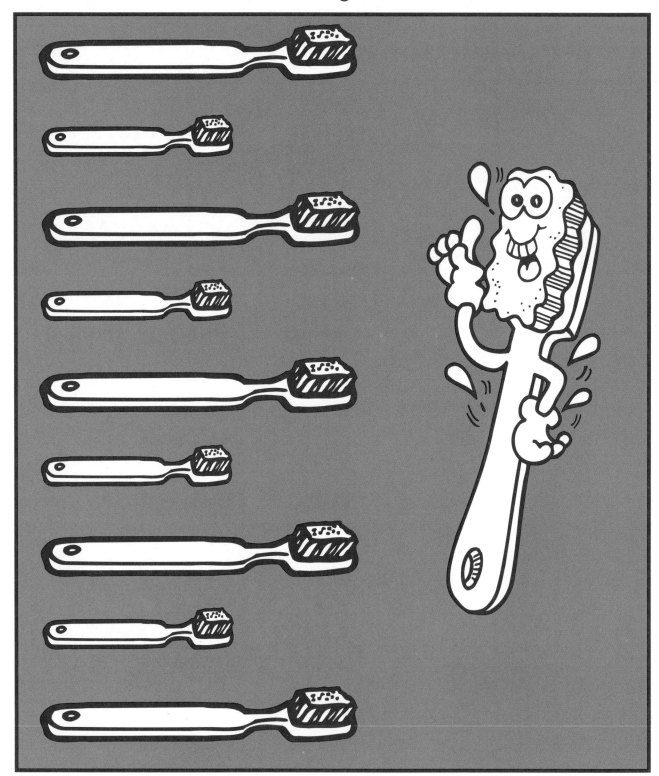

Scholastic

Draw a ◇ around the picture that is **short**.

Draw a ◇ around the picture that is **long**.

Scholastic

Circle and color the tallest sunflower yellow.
Color the other sunflowers green.

Scholastic

Draw a ◯ around the 🐱 on the **top**.

Draw a ◯ around the 🧍 on the **top**.

Draw a ◯ around the 📘 on the **bottom**.

Draw a ◯ around the 🐦 on the **bottom**.

Color the animals that are **in** their houses.

Draw a ☐ around the 🐝
above the 🌸.

Draw a ☐ around the 🐞
above the 🍃.

Draw a ☐ around the 🐰
below the 🎩.

Draw a ☐ around the 👧
below the 🪑.

Trace a  or path in each picture.

Basic Concepts Practice Test

Read the directions to your child.

1. Fill in the bubble next to the big plane.

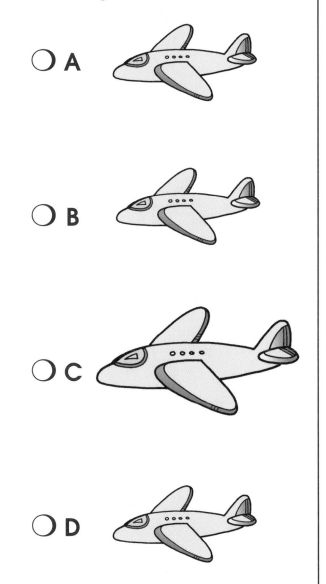

- A
- B
- C
- D

2. Fill in the bubble next to the small boat.

- F
- G
- H
- J

Basic Concepts Practice Test

Read the directions to your child.

3. Fill in the bubble next to the big car.

4. Fill in the bubble next to the small train.

○ A

○ B

○ C

○ D

○ F

○ G

○ H

○ J

Scholastic

Basic Concepts Practice Test

Read the directions to your child.

5. Fill in the bubble that shows the car that is **above** the large plane.

○ **A**

○ **B**

○ **C**

○ **D**

6. Fill in the bubble that shows the train that is **below** the large train.

○ **F**

○ **G**

○ **H**

○ **J**

Scholastic

Basic Concepts Practice Test

Read the directions to your child.

7. Fill in the bubble that shows the car that is **above** the helicopter.

⭕ A

⭕ B

⭕ C

⭕ D

8. Fill in the bubble that shows the train that is **below** the small car.

⭕ F

⭕ G

⭕ H

⭕ J

Scholastic

To **classify** means to group things that belong together.
Put an **X** on the picture that does not belong.

Scholastic

1. 2. 3. 4. 5. 6. 7. Example

 and  are the **same**.

Connect the cars that are the same.

 Name one way you and a friend are the same.

Scholastic

 and are **different**.

Circle the plane that is different in each row.

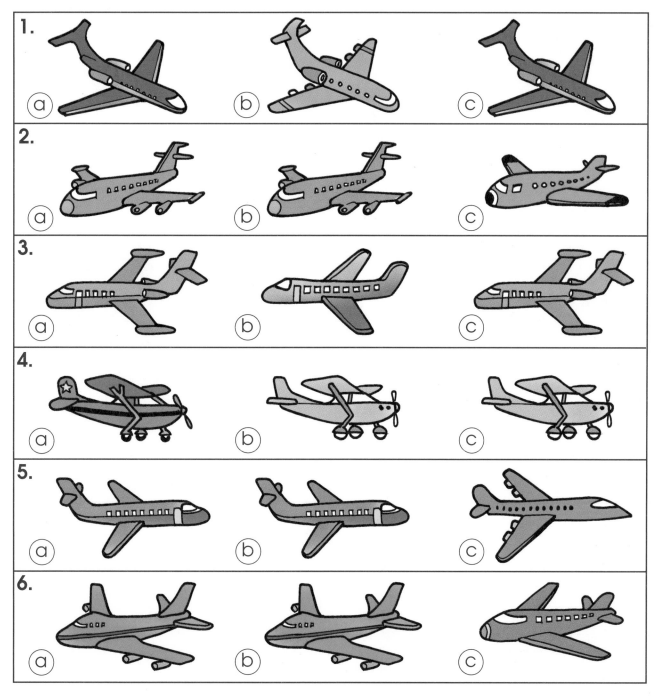

1.
ⓐ ⓑ ⓒ

2.
ⓐ ⓑ ⓒ

3.
ⓐ ⓑ ⓒ

4.
ⓐ ⓑ ⓒ

5.
ⓐ ⓑ ⓒ

6.
ⓐ ⓑ ⓒ

 Name one way you and a friend are different.

Circle the objects that are the same in each box.

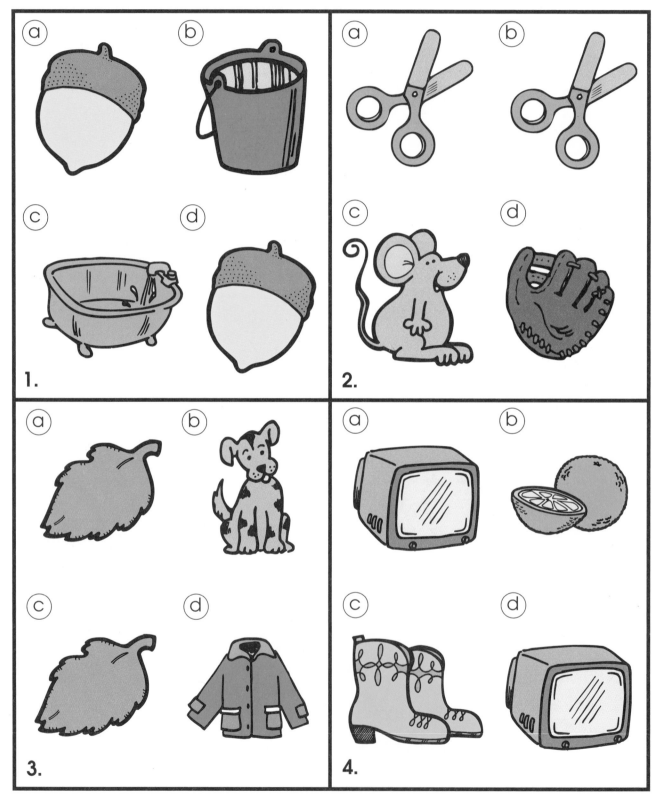

1.

2.

3.

4.

Scholastic

Circle the objects that are the same in each box.

1.
2.
3.
4.

Circle the objects in each row that are the same as the first one.

Draw a line to match the objects that are the same.

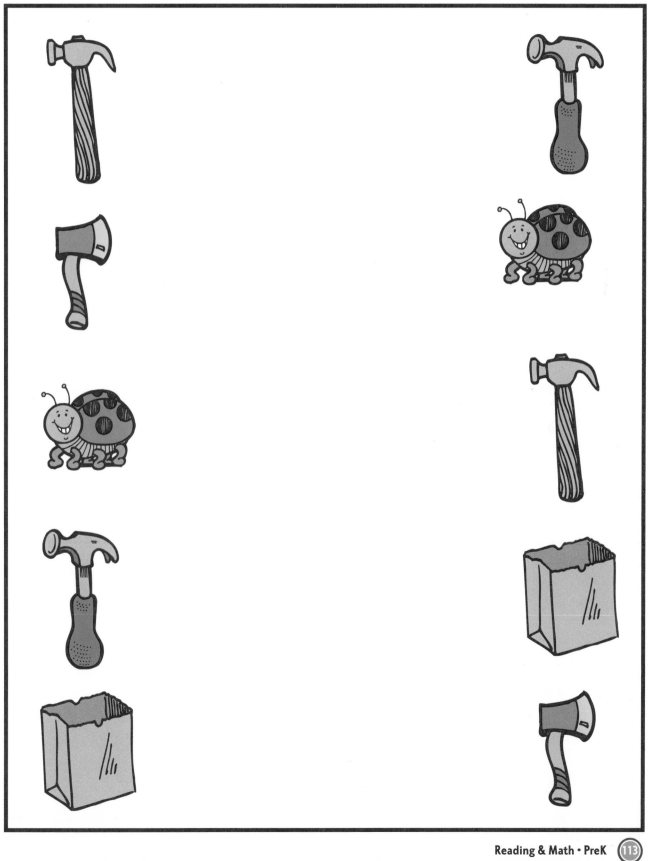

Draw a line to match the objects that are the same.

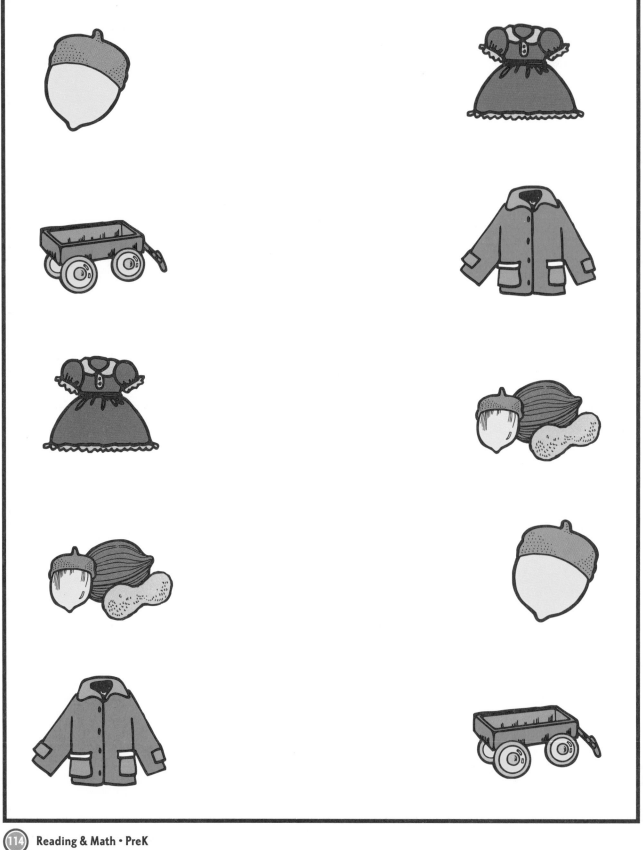

Scholastic

Circle the object that is different in each box.

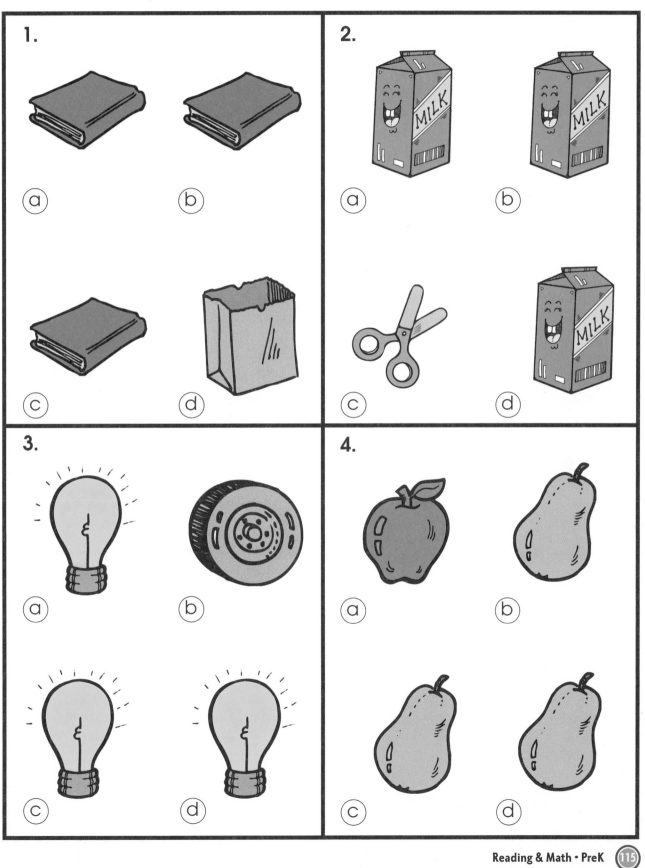

1.
a
b
c
d

2.
a
b
c
d

3.
a
b
c
d

4.
a
b
c
d

Circle the object that is different in each row.

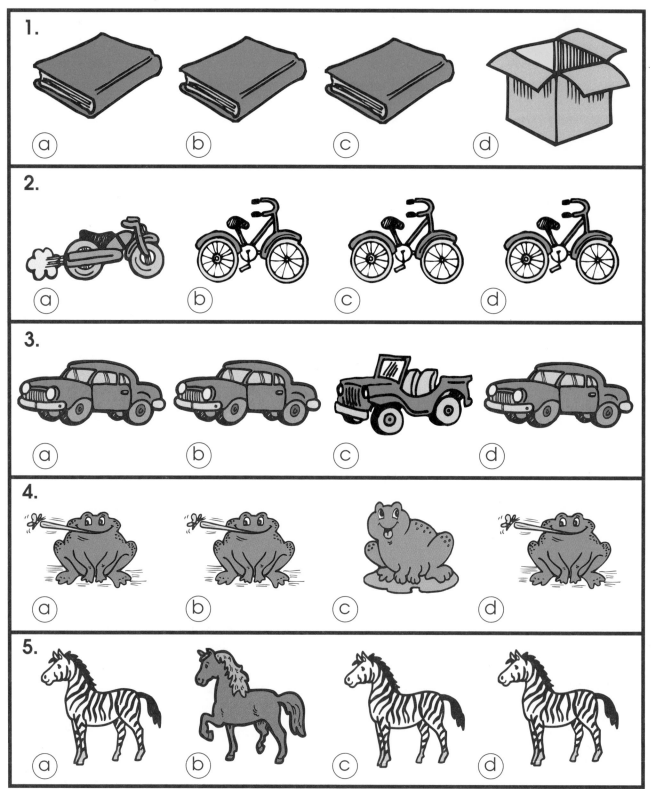

1. a b c d

2. a b c d

3. a b c d

4. a b c d

5. a b c d

Things that are **pretend** are **not real**.
Circle 5 pretend things in the picture.

Things that are **pretend** are **not real**.

Color the real pictures.
Do not color the pretend pictures.

1.

2.

Scholastic

Reading Readiness Practice Test

Read the directions to your child.

1. Fill in the bubble next to the picture that is different.

○ **A**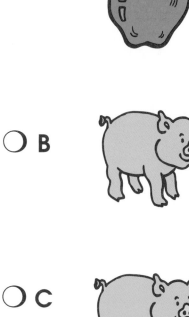

○ **B**

○ **C**

○ **D**

2. Fill in the bubble next to the picture that is different.

○ **F**

○ **G**

○ **H**

○ **J**

Reading Readiness Practice Test

Read the directions to your child.

3. Fill in the bubble next to the picture that is different.

○ A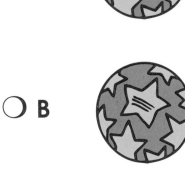

○ B

○ C

○ D

4. Fill in the bubble next to the picture that does not belong.

○ F

○ G

○ H

○ J

Scholastic

Reading Readiness Practice Test

Read the directions to your child.

5. Fill in the bubble next to the picture that does not belong.

○ A

○ B

○ C

○ D

6. Fill in the bubble next to the picture that does not belong.

○ F

○ G

○ H

○ J

Scholastic

Reading Readiness Practice Test

Read the directions to your child.

7. Fill in the bubble next to the object that is different.

○ **A**
○ **B**
○ **C**
○ **D**

8. Fill in the bubble next to the object that is different.

○ **F**
○ **G**
○ **H**
○ **J**

Scholastic

Thinking Skills

Developing problem-solving strategies and logical reasoning, being able to distinguish similarities and differences, and recognizing relationships between items are all important school-readiness skills.

What to Do

Read the directions on each page to your child. When finished, help your child check his or her work. Offer lots of praise for being such a "terrific thinker!"

Keep On Going!

• Work thinking skills into everyday conversations. For instance, in the supermarket, you might say, "In the basket we have an apple, an orange, and a loaf of bread. Which one is not like the others?"

• When your child expresses a desire for something, help him or her label it as a "need" or a "want."

Circle the three pictures that belong together in each row.

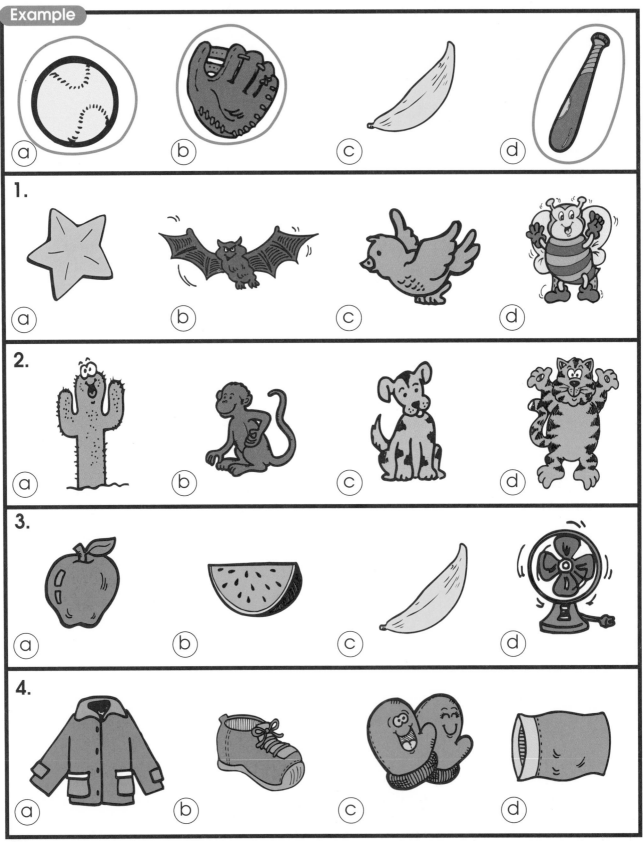

Example

a. b. c. d.

1.

a. b. c. d.

2.

a. b. c. d.

3.

a. b. c. d.

4.

a. b. c. d.

Scholastic

Circle the pictures that belong together in each box.

1.

2.

3.

4.

Circle the pictures that belong together in each row.

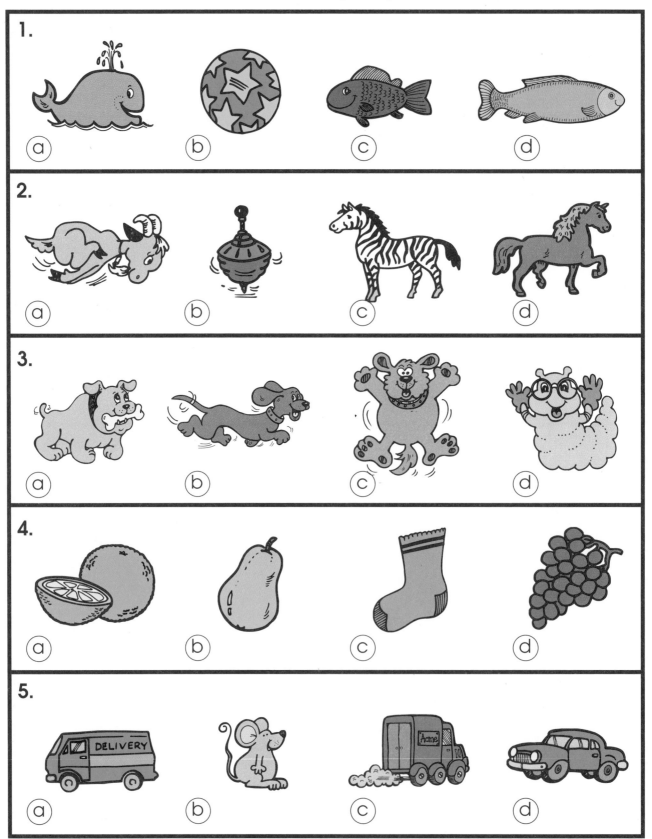

1. ⓐ ⓑ ⓒ ⓓ

2. ⓐ ⓑ ⓒ ⓓ

3. ⓐ ⓑ ⓒ ⓓ

4. ⓐ ⓑ ⓒ ⓓ

5. ⓐ ⓑ ⓒ ⓓ

Scholastic

Draw a line to match the pictures that go together.

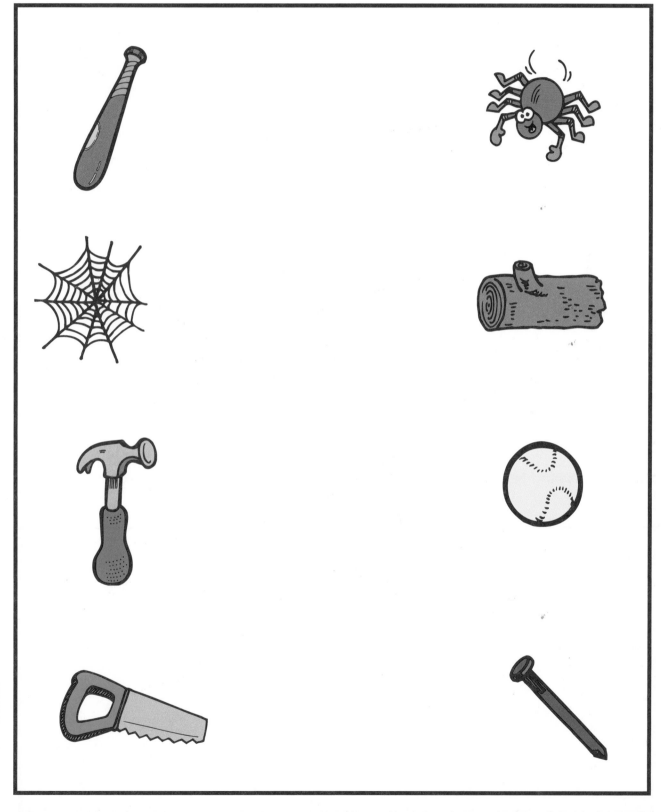

Draw a line to match the pictures that go together.

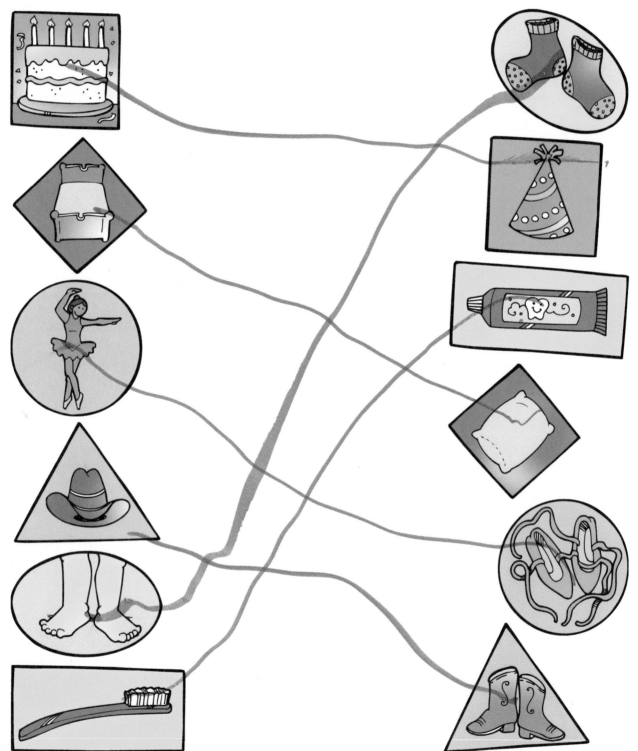

Put an **X** on the object that does not belong in each box.

1.
a
b
c
d

2.
a
b
c
d

3.
a
b
c
d

4.
a
b
c
d

Circle the picture that goes with the first picture in each row.

Scholastic

Draw a line to match the workers to their tools.

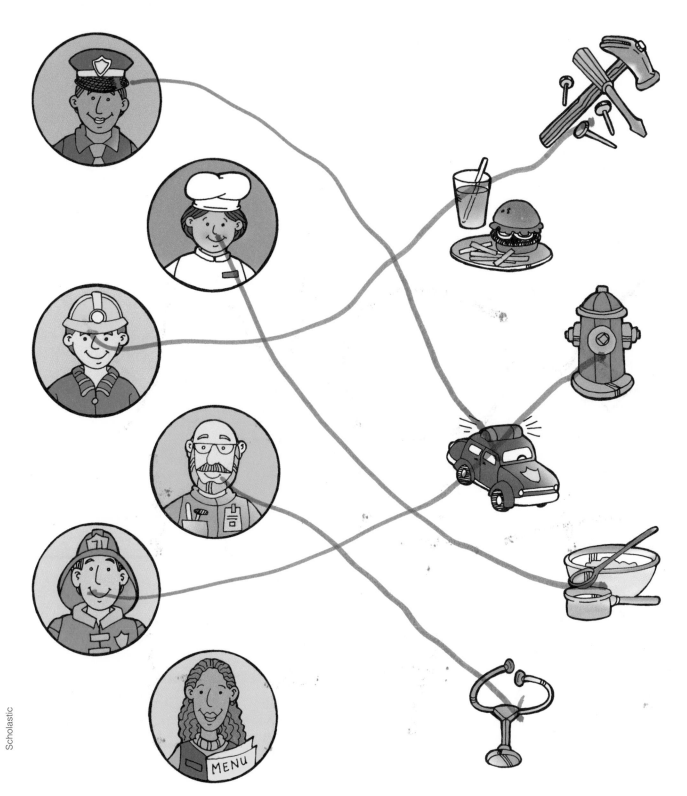

We wear different kinds of clothes for
different weather.

(1) **Look** at the pictures.

(2) **Draw** a circle around the picture in each row
that does not belong.

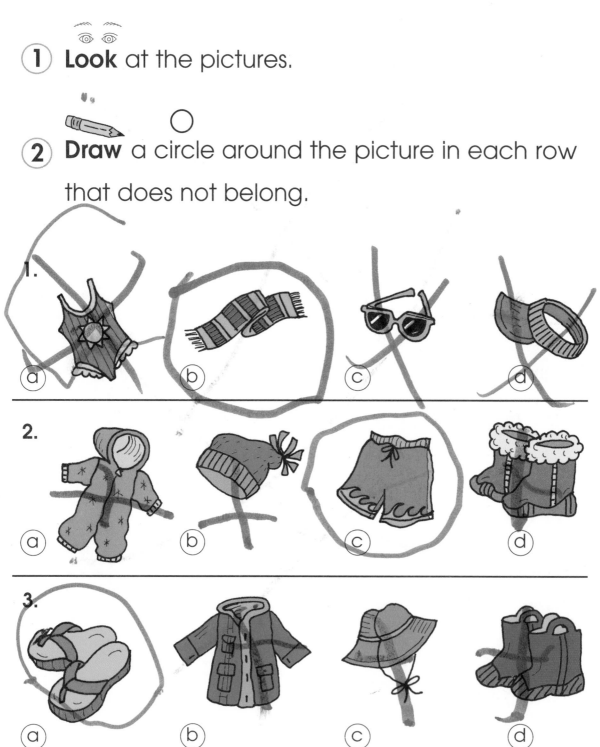

1.
(a) (b) (c) (d)

2.
(a) (b) (c) (d)

3.
(a) (b) (c) (d)

Scholastic

You can do different things in different seasons.

1 **Look** at the pictures.

2 **Draw** lines to match the children with each season.

A **want** is something we do not need but enjoy having.
A toy is a want.

Draw an **X** on each want.

Transportation is how we get from one place to another.

Color the transportation for land green.
Color the transportation for water blue.
Color the transportation for air purple.

Scholastic

People use **tools** to do work.

Color the tool in each row that the worker needs.

 Talk about what you want to be when you grow up.

Scholastic

Thinking Skills Practice Test

Read the directions to your child.

1. Fill in the bubble next to the picture that does not belong.

○ **A**

○ **B**

● **C**

○ **D**

2. Fill in the bubble next to the picture that does not belong.

● **F**

○ **G**

○ **H**

○ **J**

Scholastic

Thinking Skills Practice Test

Read the directions to your child.

3. Fill in the bubble next to the picture that does not belong.

○ A

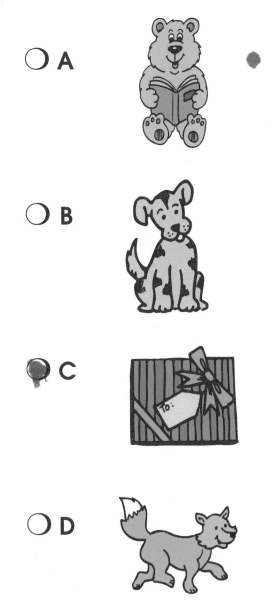

○ B

● C

○ D

4. Fill in the bubble next to the picture that does not belong.

○ F

○ G

○ H

● J

Scholastic

Thinking Skills Practice Test

Read the directions to your child.

5. Fill in the bubble next to the picture that does not belong.

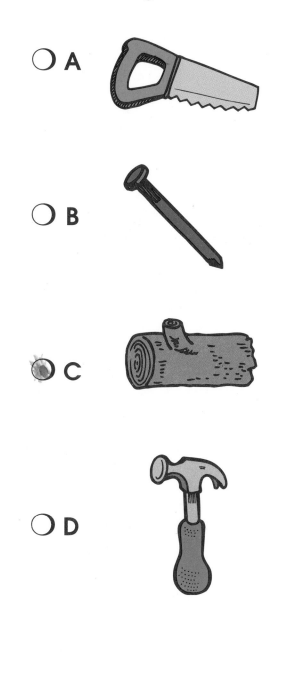

○ A

○ B

◉ C

○ D

6. Fill in the bubble next to the picture that does not belong.

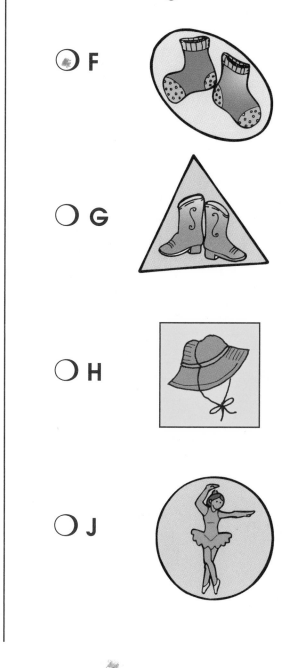

◉ F

○ G

○ H

○ J

Scholastic

Thinking Skills Practice Test

Read the directions to your child.

7. Fill in the bubble next to the thing that shows something you **need**.

○ A

○ B

○ C

○ D

8. Fill in the bubble next to the thing that shows something you **want**.

○ F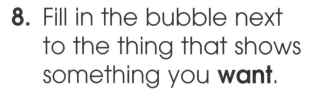

○ G

○ H

○ J

Scholastic

Word Building

Building a strong vocabulary is an important step in becoming a strong reader. Many of the words your child will practice in this section are the most commonly encountered words in print. Recognizing them quickly will help children become better readers.

What to Do
You'll find many of the words from this section on pages 271–284 in the Flash Card section. Use the cards to review the words with your child. You can also use them to build sentences together.

Keep On Going!
Have your child add new word cards as he or she learns new words at home and in school.

Trace the word **red**.

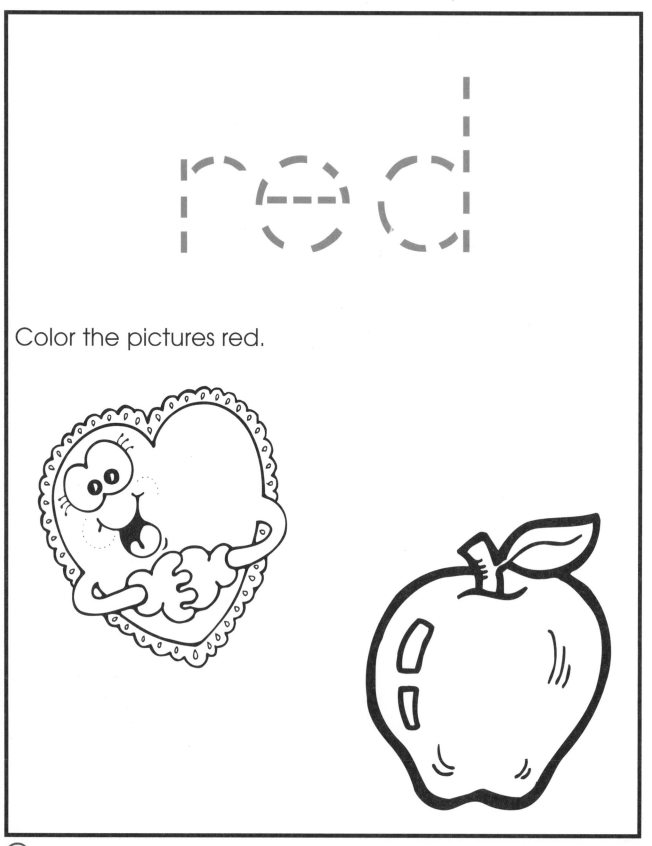

Color the pictures red.

Trace and write the word **red**.

red

Draw and color a picture of something red.

Scholastic

Trace the word **blue**.

Color the pictures blue.

Trace and write the word **blue**.

blue

Draw and color a picture of something blue.

Scholastic

Trace the word **orange**.

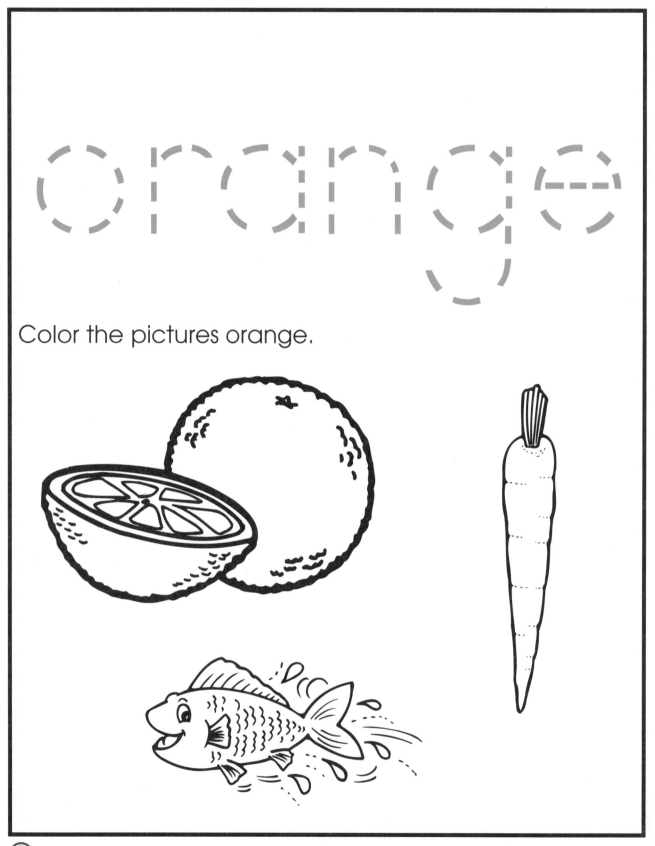

Color the pictures orange.

Trace and write the word **orange**.

orange

Draw and color a picture of something orange.

Trace the word **yellow**.

Color the pictures yellow.

SCHOOL BUS

Trace and write the word **yellow**.

yellow

Draw and color a picture of something yellow.

Trace the word **black**.

Color the pictures black.

Trace and write the word **black**.

Draw and color a picture of something black.

Trace the word **green**.

Color the pictures green.

Scholastic

Trace and write the word **green**.

green

Draw and color a picture of something green.

Clowning Around

Color.

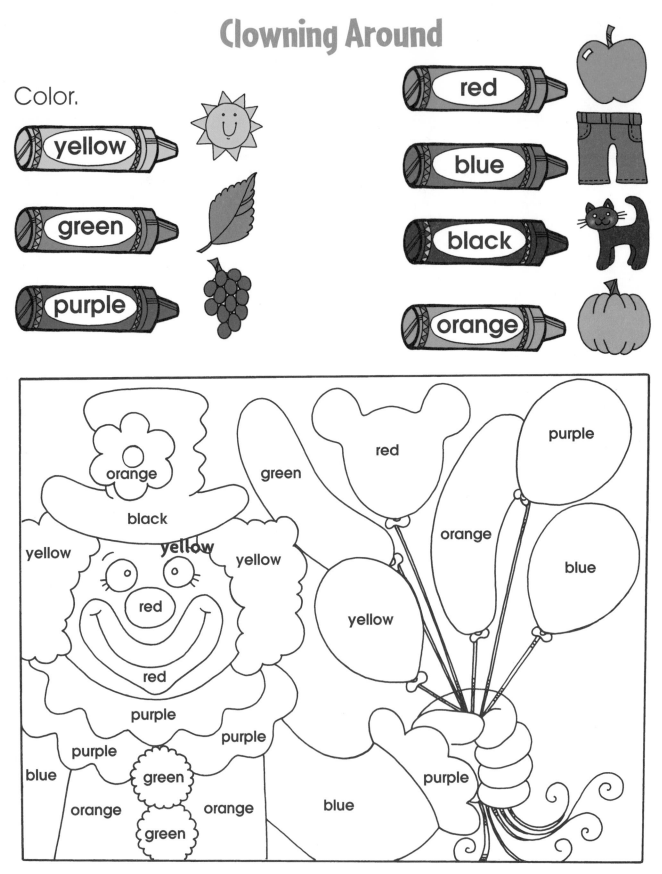

Scholastic

Circle the picture that shows the **opposite**.

1. big   ⓐ little ⓑ

2. in   ⓐ out ⓑ

3. hot   ⓐ cold ⓑ

4. full   ⓐ empty ⓑ

This butterfly is **large**. This butterfly is **small**.
Circle the large item on each petal.

 Name two things that are larger than you.

Scholastic

This duck is **over**.   This duck is **under**.

Circle the correct answer.

1. Where do you see more ducks? over under

2. Where do you see more frogs? over under

This animal is **in**.  This animal is **out**.

Color each animal that is in its home.

This star is **right** of the moon.

This star is **left** of the moon.

Color each ⭐ that is right of the moon yellow.

Color each ⭐ that is left of the moon orange.

Scholastic

Circle the picture that shows the opposite.

1. full — a) empty b)

2. loud — a) quiet b)

3. slow — a) fast b)

4. over — a) under b)

5. wet — a) dry b)

Scholastic

The **body** is made up of many parts.
Draw a line to each body part.

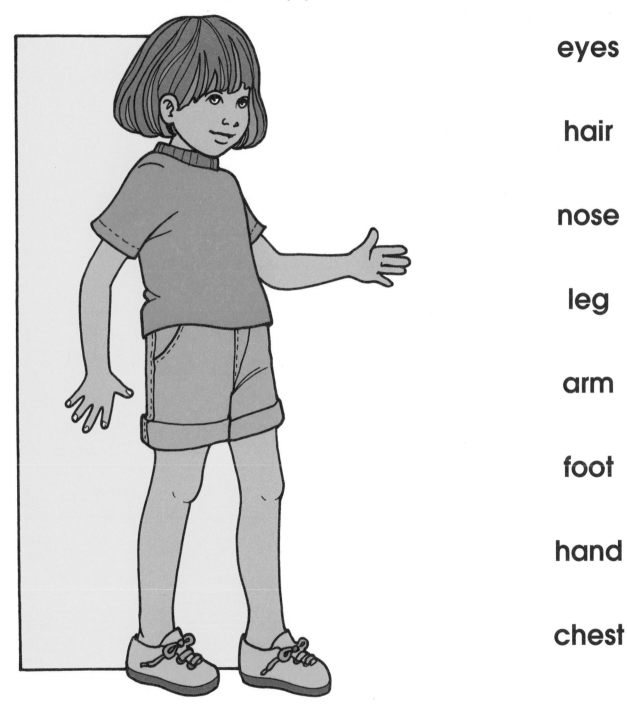

eyes

hair

nose

leg

arm

foot

hand

chest

 Name three other body parts.

Scholastic

We use our **senses** to learn about new things.

We **see** with our .

We **hear** with our .

We **smell** with our .

We **taste** with our .

We **touch** with our .

Look at each picture. Circle the senses you would use.

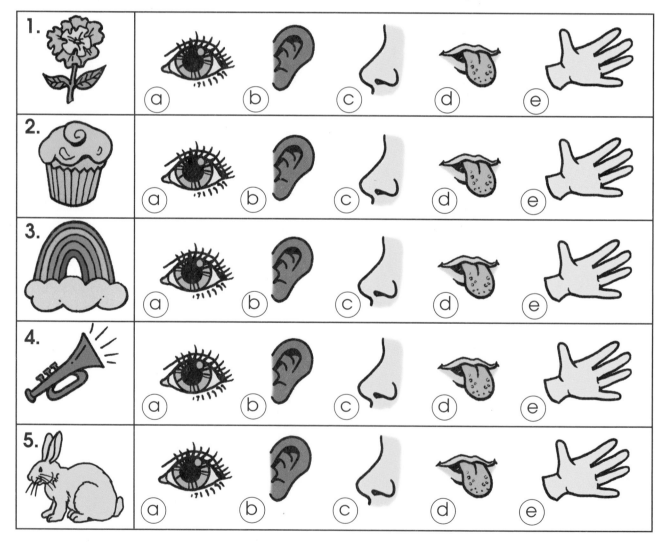

Scholastic

A **need** is something we must have to live. Food, clothing, and a place to live are needs.

Connect the dots. Color.

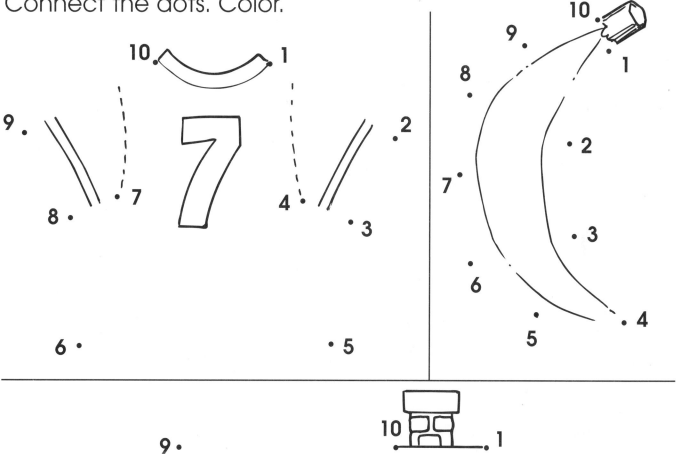

Scholastic

We wear **clothes** to go with the weather.
Connect the top, bottom, and shoes that go together.

Scholastic

Say the numbers for each **phone number**. Push the buttons and pretend to call each one.

437-6055

506-1187

916-5432

537-4906

190-3587

Write your phone number in the boxes.

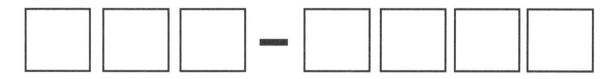

Color the numbers in your phone number on the phone above.

 Do you know to dial 9-1-1 for an emergency?

Word Building Practice Test

Read the directions to your child.

1. Fill in the bubble next to the picture you would color **red**.

◯ A

◯ B

◯ C

◯ D

2. Fill in the bubble next to the picture you would color **orange**.

◯ F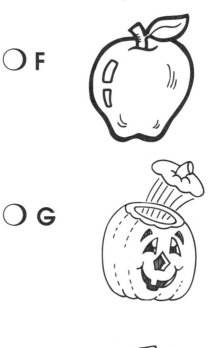

◯ G

◯ H

◯ J

Word Building Practice Test

Read the directions to your child.

3. Fill in the bubble next to the picture you would **not** color yellow.

○ A

○ B

○ C

○ D

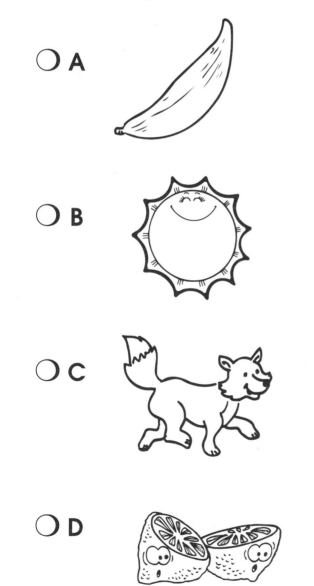

4. Fill in the bubble next to the picture you would **not** color green.

○ F

○ G

○ H

○ J

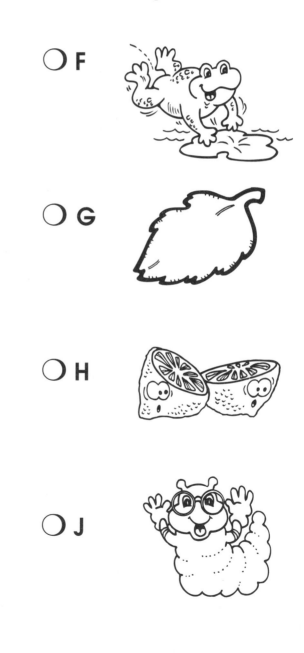

Word Building Practice Test

Read the directions to your child.

5. Fill in the bubble next to the picture that is opposite of **happy**.

○ **A**

○ **B**

○ **C**

○ **D**

6. Fill in the bubble next to the picture that is opposite of **up**.

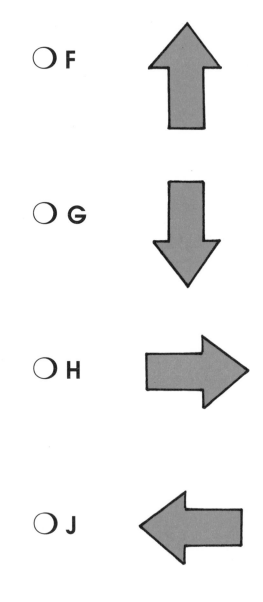

○ **F**

○ **G**

○ **H**

○ **J**

Scholastic

Word Building Practice Test

Read the directions to your child.

7. Fill in the bubble next to the sense you would use when you see a turtle.

○ A

○ B

○ C

○ D

8. Fill in the bubble next to the sense you would use when you listen to music.

○ F

○ G

○ H

○ J

Scholastic

Numbers & Number Concepts

Recognizing and writing numerals, counting, and counting by groups ("skip-counting") are crucial to children's early math learning. In addition, concepts like "more than," "less than," "equal," and identifying quantities of items are all key to math success.

What to Do

Read the directions on each page to your child. Some of the activities require scissors and paste. When he or she is finished, help your child check his or her work. Offer lots of praise for being such a "marvelous mathematician!"

Keep on Going!

Count everything around you—wheels on a car, stripes on a shirt, sections of an orange!

one

Number Practice

Trace the number.

Write the number.

Trace the word.

one one one one

Write the word.

Number Hunt

Circle every number 1.

6	3	1	8	9	22	8	30	0	1	27
20	2	4	6	1	5	9	1	5	26	3
5	22	6	7	8	1	27	0	3	4	1
1	23	8	1	29	0	4	7	9	3	1

Scholastic

Cut out 1 sun. Paste it in the sky.

the number

one

Draw 1 rainbow.

2

two

Number Practice

Trace the number.

2 2 2 2 2 2 2 2

Write the number.

Trace the word.

two two two two

Write the word.

Number Hunt

Circle every number 2.

13	0	4	6	19	2	30	2	0	17
2	9	3	14	0	2	11	5	6	15
17	3	2	6	16	8	10	7	9	2
19	2	18	9	5	4	2	0	1	16

Cut out 2 trees. Paste them on the hill.

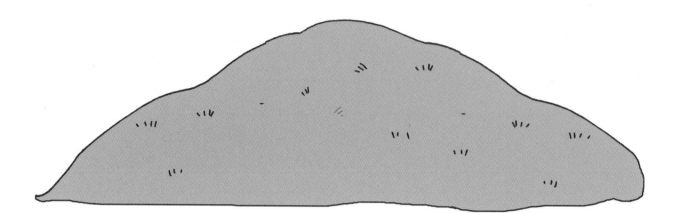

Draw 2 birds in the nest.

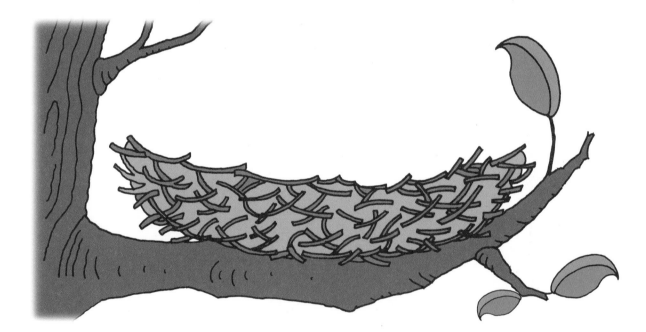

Scholastic

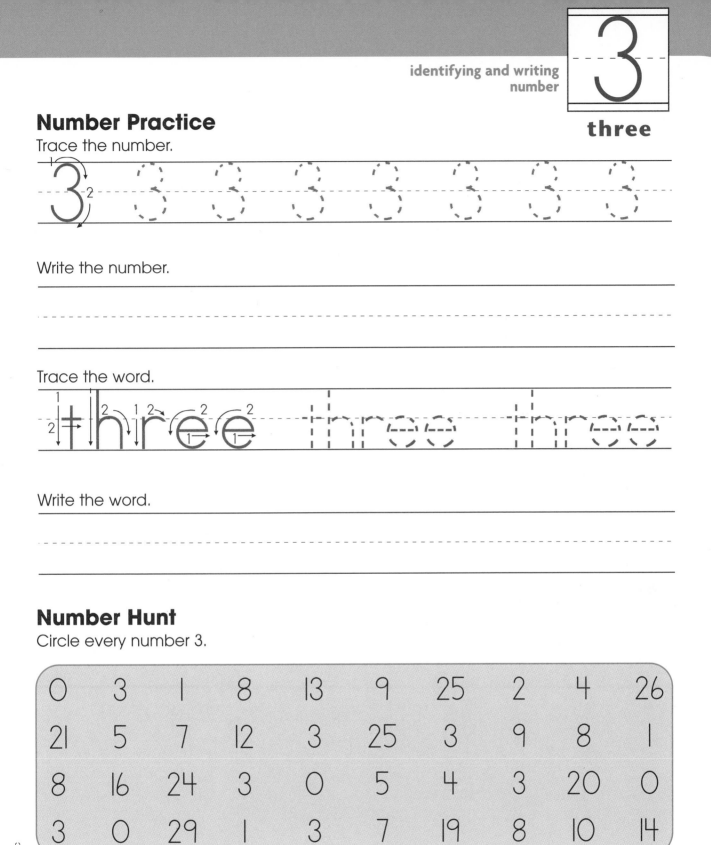

Number Practice

Trace the number.

Write the number.

Trace the word.

Write the word.

Number Hunt

Circle every number 3.

0	3	1	8	13	9	25	2	4	26
21	5	7	12	3	25	3	9	8	1
8	16	24	3	0	5	4	3	20	0
3	0	29	1	3	7	19	8	10	14

Scholastic

Cut out 3 goldfish. Paste them in the bowl.

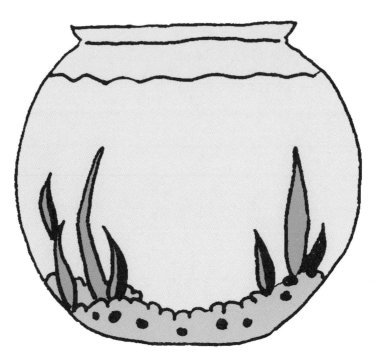

Draw 3 whales in the ocean.

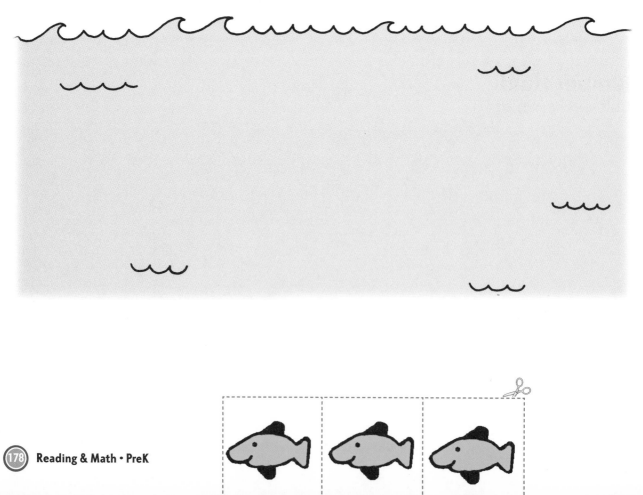

Scholastic

Number Practice

Trace the number.

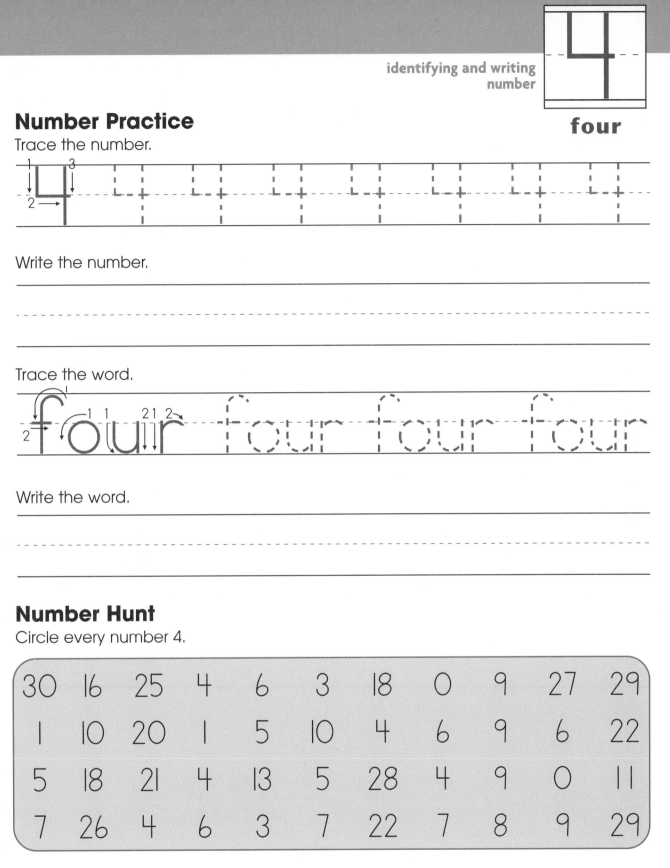

Write the number.

Trace the word.

Write the word.

Number Hunt

Circle every number 4.

30	16	25	4	6	3	18	0	9	27	29
1	10	20	1	5	10	4	6	9	6	22
5	18	21	4	13	5	28	4	9	0	11
7	26	4	6	3	7	22	7	8	9	29

Scholastic

Cut out 4 crabs. Paste them on the beach.

Draw 4 beach balls.

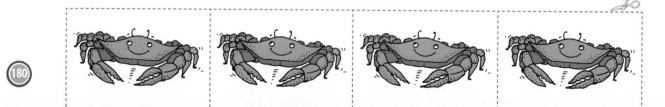

five

Number Practice

Trace the number.

Write the number.

Trace the word.

Write the word.

Number Hunt

Circle every number 5.

2	5	3	0	1	4	5	8	9	6	10
6	4	18	5	2	1	7	5	0	9	5
7	3	8	1	9	5	16	7	0	1	4
11	4	5	9	21	3	9	2	1	10	8

Cut out 5 butterflies. Paste them in the garden.

Draw 5 ladybugs on the leaf.

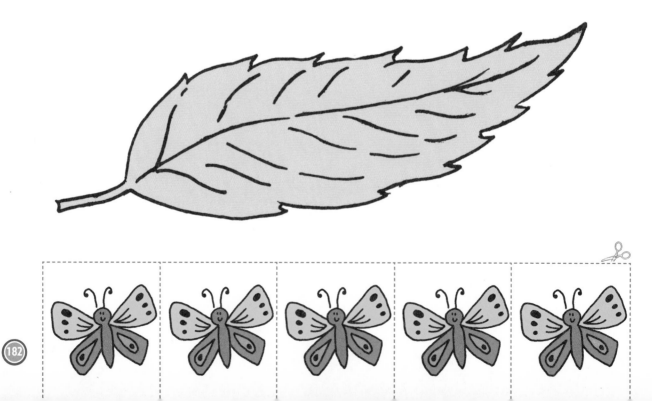

Number Practice

Trace the number.

6 6 6 6 6 6 6 6

Write the number.

Trace the word.

six six six six six

Write the word.

Number Hunt

Circle every number 6.

0	2	1	8	13	9	25	2	6	20	5
28	6	7	12	9	25	3	6	8	1	9
6	17	2	6	3	0	5	6	3	20	0
0	29	1	3	7	19	8	10	1	6	8

Scholastic

Cut out 6 frogs. Paste them on the log.

Draw 6 flies for the frogs to eat.

Number Practice

Trace the number.

Write the number.

Trace the word.

Write the word.

Number Hunt

Circle every number 7.

5	7	1	8	13	9	25	7	4	26
11	5	7	12	3	25	3	9	8	1
2	16	24	3	7	5	4	3	20	0
8	7	29	1	3	7	19	8	10	14

Scholastic

Cut out 7 lollipops. Paste them in the candy jar.

Draw 7 candles on the cake.

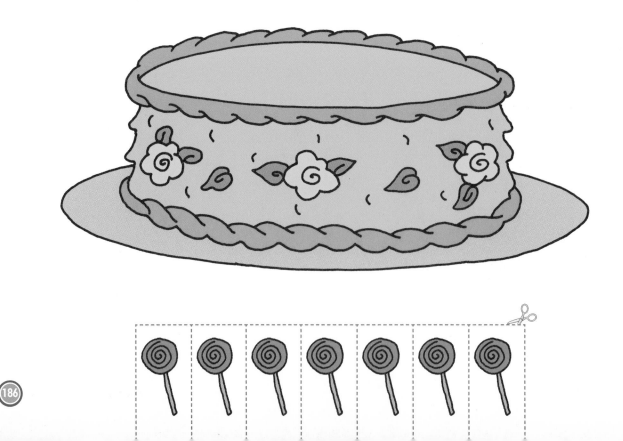

Number Practice

Trace the number.

8 8 8 8 8 8 8 8

Write the number.

Trace the word.

eight   eight   eight

Write the word.

Number Hunt

Circle every number 8.

9	25	2	4	26	8	13	4	0	8
12	3	25	3	9	21	5	7	8	1
24	8	0	5	4	3	20	0	5	8
1	8	7	19	8	10	14	9	3	0

Scholastic

Cut out 8 lizards. Paste them on the rock.

Draw 8 spiders on the web.

Scholastic

Number Practice

Trace the number.

q q q q q q q q

Write the number.

Trace the word.

nine nine nine nine

Write the word.

Number Hunt

Circle every number 9.

9	3	1	8	13	9	25	2	4	26
8	1	2	21	5	7	12	3	25	3
0	9	4	3	20	0	9	8	16	24
1	7	20	8	10	3	0	2	9	14

Scholastic

Cut out **9** sheep. Paste them in the field.

Draw **9** clouds in the sky.

Scholastic

10

ten

Number Practice

Trace the number.

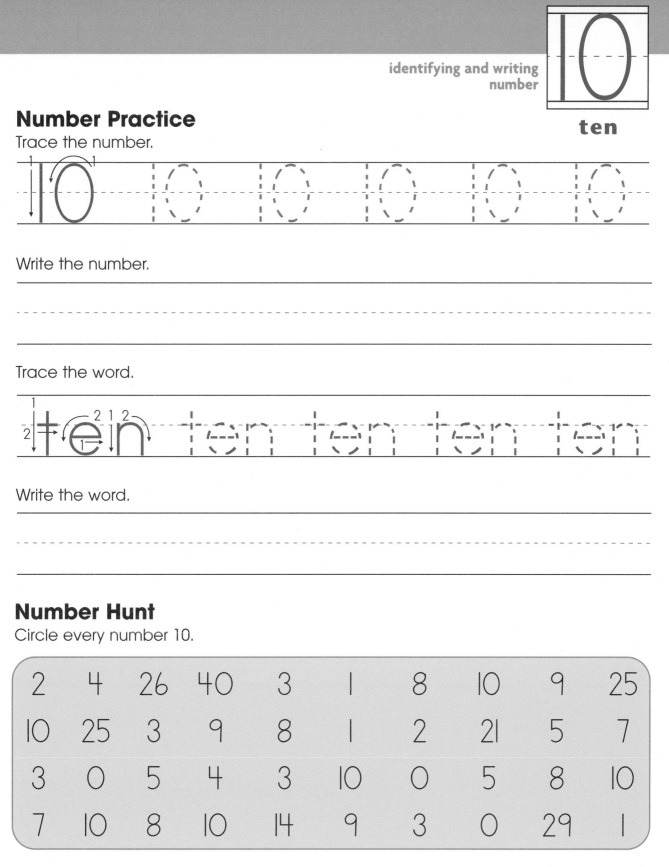

Write the number.

Trace the word.

Write the word.

Number Hunt

Circle every number 10.

2	4	26	40	3	1	8	10	9	25
10	25	3	9	8	1	2	21	5	7
3	0	5	4	3	10	0	5	8	10
7	10	8	10	14	9	3	0	29	1

Cut out 10 owls. Paste them on the branches.

Draw 10 bats in the cave.

Scholastic

Color.

one = yellow   two = black   three = blue

four = white   five = orange   six = green

seven = red   eight = purple   nine = brown

ten = pink

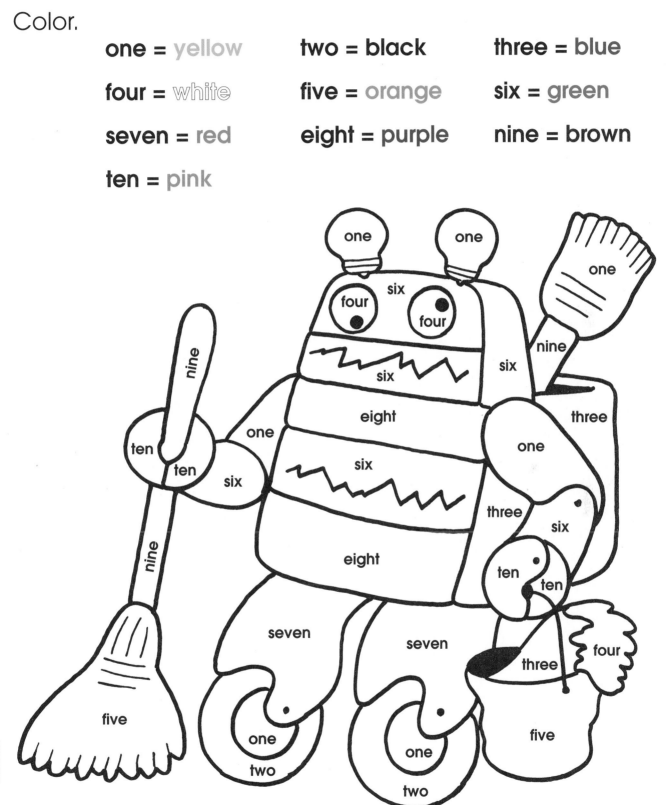

How many of each kind of animal do you see?

1 **Count** each kind of animal.

2 **Write** the number in the box.

Scholastic

Draw a circle around each group of 1.
Draw a box around each group of 2.

1.

2.

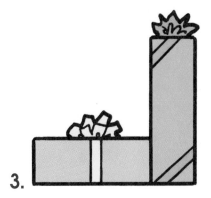

3.

4.

5.

6.

7.

8.

9.

Scholastic

Draw a circle around each group of 3.
Draw a box around each group of 4.

1.

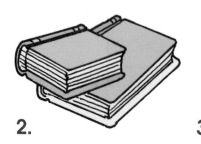

2.

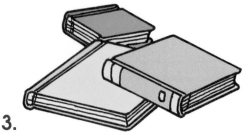

3.

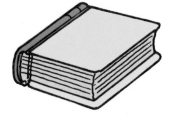

4.

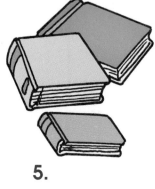

5.

6.

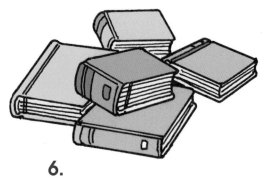

7.

8.

9.

Scholastic

Draw a circle around each group of 5.
Draw a box around each group of 6.

1.

2.

3.

4.

5.

6.

7.

8.

9.

Scholastic

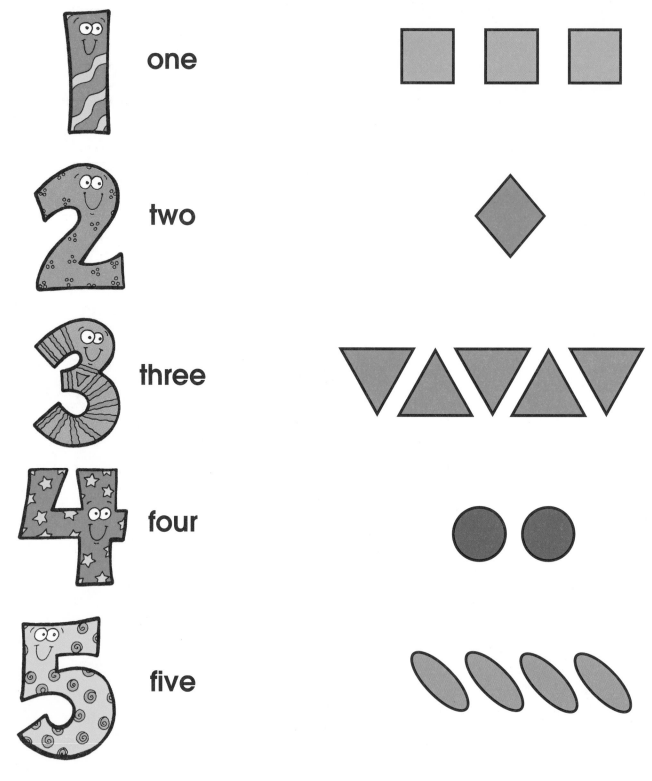

Draw a line to match each number to the set of shapes.

one

two

three

four

five

Color each group of 7 red.
Color each group of 8 yellow.

1.

2.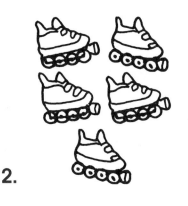

3.

4.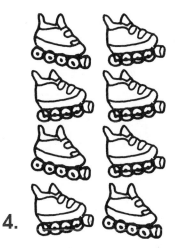

5.

6.

7.

8.

9.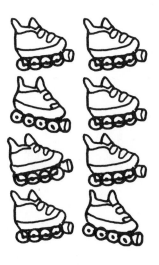

Scholastic

Color each group of 9 blue.
Color each group of 10 green.

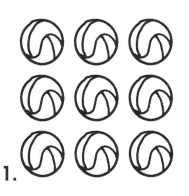

1.

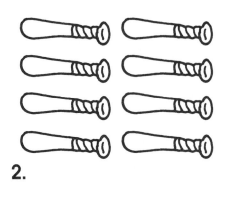

2.

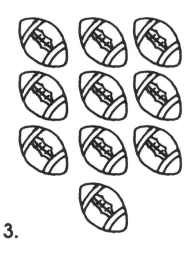

3.

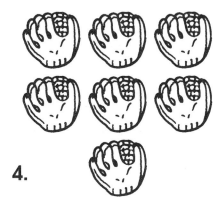

4.

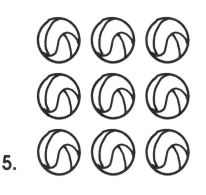

5.

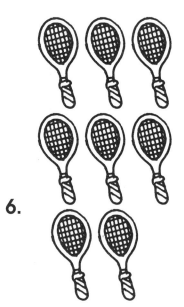

6.

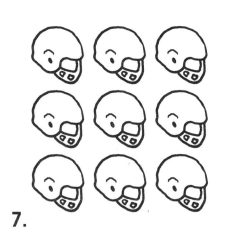

7.

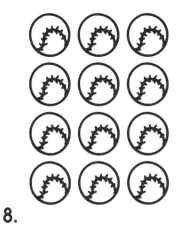

8.

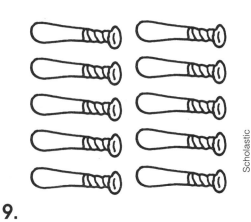

9.

Scholastic

Circle the correct number of objects.

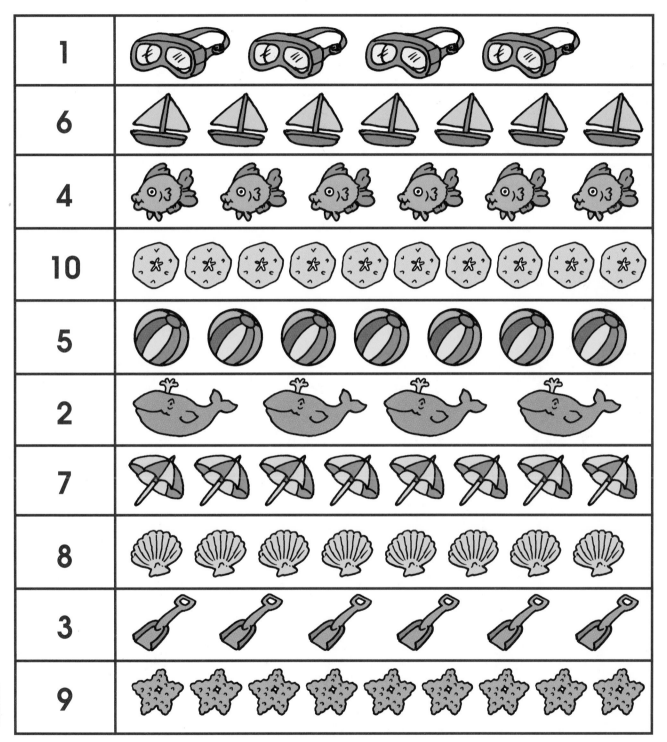

1	
6	
4	
10	
5	
2	
7	
8	
3	
9	

Color.

⠂⠂	blue	⠈⠂⠂	red	⠒⠒	green
orange		purple		black	
brown		white		yellow	

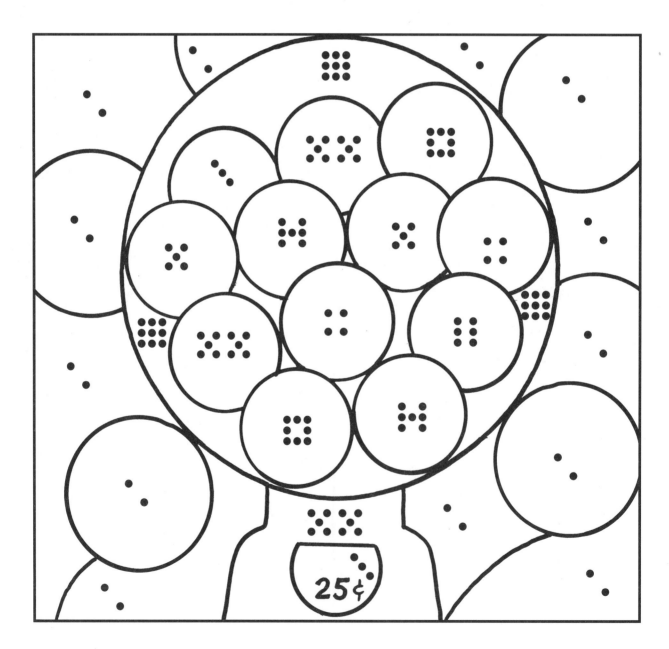

Scholastic

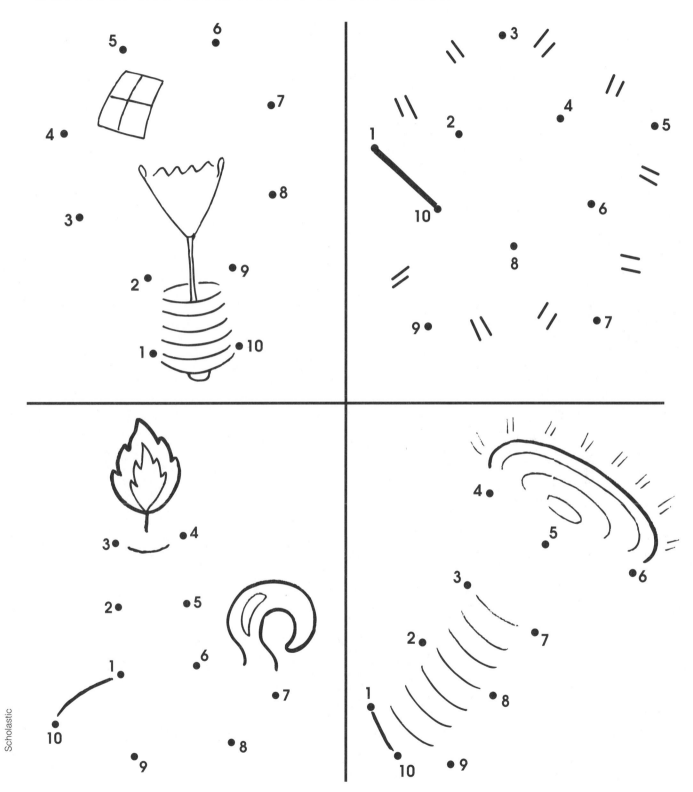

Connect the dots from **1** to **10**. Color.

Write each missing number.

Circle the pictures with the same number as in the first picture.

Draw a line to match the groups with the same number.

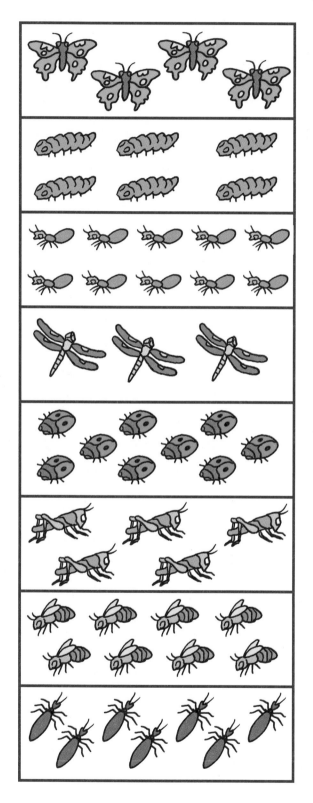 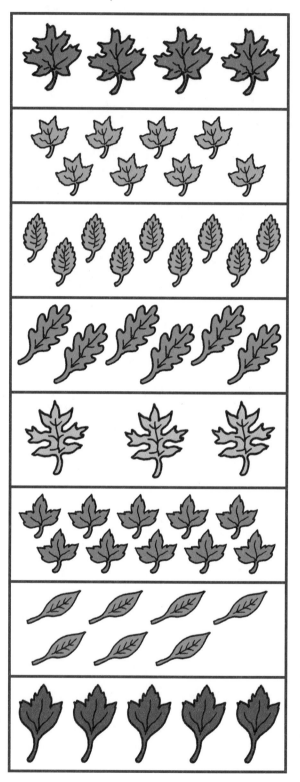

Scholastic

Circle the one with more.

1.
   (a)   (b)

2.
   (a)   (b)

3.
   (a)   (b)

4.
   (a)   (b)

5.
   (a)   (b)

Scholastic

Color the dog with more spots in each picture.

Circle the one with less in each box.

Numbers & Number Concepts Practice Test

Read the directions to your child.

1. Count the number of objects. Fill in the bubble next to the correct number.

○ **A** 1
○ **B** 2
○ **C** 3
○ **D** 4

2. Count the number of objects. Fill in the bubble next to the correct number.

○ **F** 1
○ **G** 2
○ **H** 3
○ **J** 4

Scholastic

Numbers & Number Concepts Practice Test

Read the directions to your child.

3. Count the number of objects. Fill in the bubble next to the correct number.

○ **A**   1

○ **B**   2

○ **C**   3

○ **D**   4

4. Count the number of objects. Fill in the bubble next to the correct number.

○ **F**   1

○ **G**   3

○ **H**   4

○ **J**   5

Scholastic

Numbers & Number Concepts Practice Test

Read the directions to your child.

5. Count the number of objects in the group. Fill in the bubble next to the correct number.

    ○ **A**   7

    ○ **B**   8

    ○ **C**   9

    ○ **D**   10

6. Count the number of objects in the group. Fill in the bubble next to the correct number.

    ○ **F**   5

    ○ **G**   6

    ○ **H**   7

    ○ **J**   8

Read the directions to your child.

7. Count the number of objects in the group.
Fill in the bubble next to the correct number.

○ **A** 7

○ **B** 8

○ **C** 9

○ **D** 10

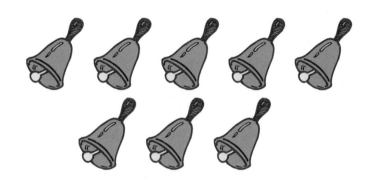

8. Count the number of objects in the group. Fill in the bubble next to the correct number.

○ **F** 7

○ **G** 8

○ **H** 9

○ **J** 10

Scholastic

Shapes

Recognizing shapes is the basic foundation of geometry skills. Being able to draw shapes helps children develop fine motor skills and also the basic strokes used in letter formation.

What to Do

Read the directions on each page to your child. When he or she is finished, help your child check his or her work. Offer lots of praise for being such a "super shape kid!"

Keep On Going!

• Challenge your child to find certain shapes around them; for instance, wheels, clocks, and lights on a stoplight are all circles.

• Cut colored paper into different shapes and have your child paste them onto a larger sheet of paper to make a shape collage.

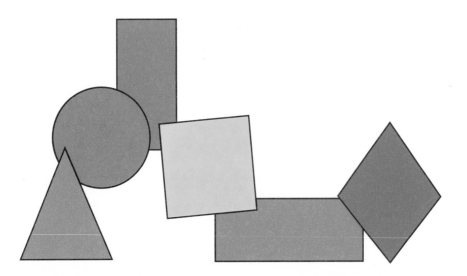

Trace and color the circles.

Scholastic

Color all of the circles red.

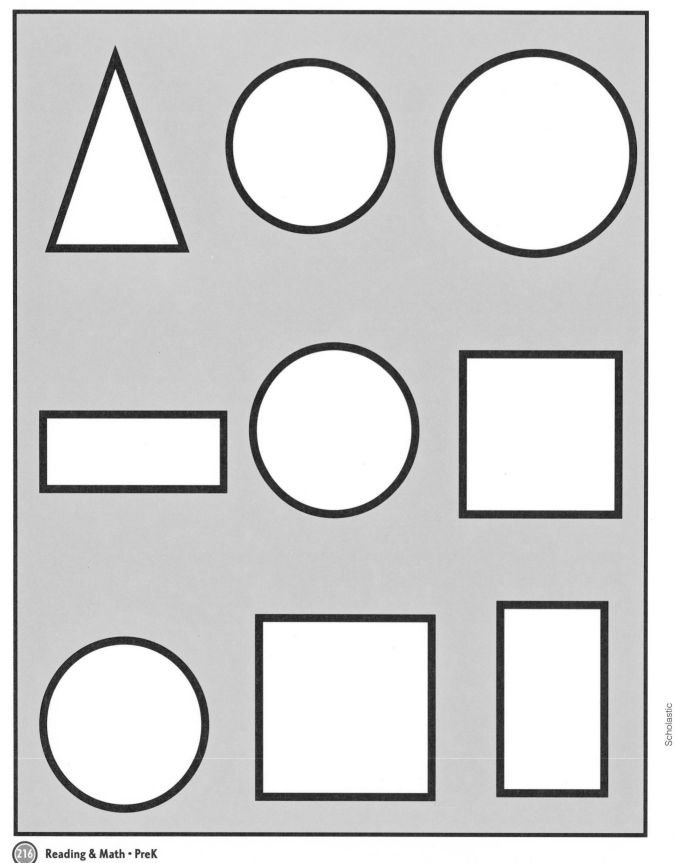

Scholastic

Trace the balls. Draw four more balls.

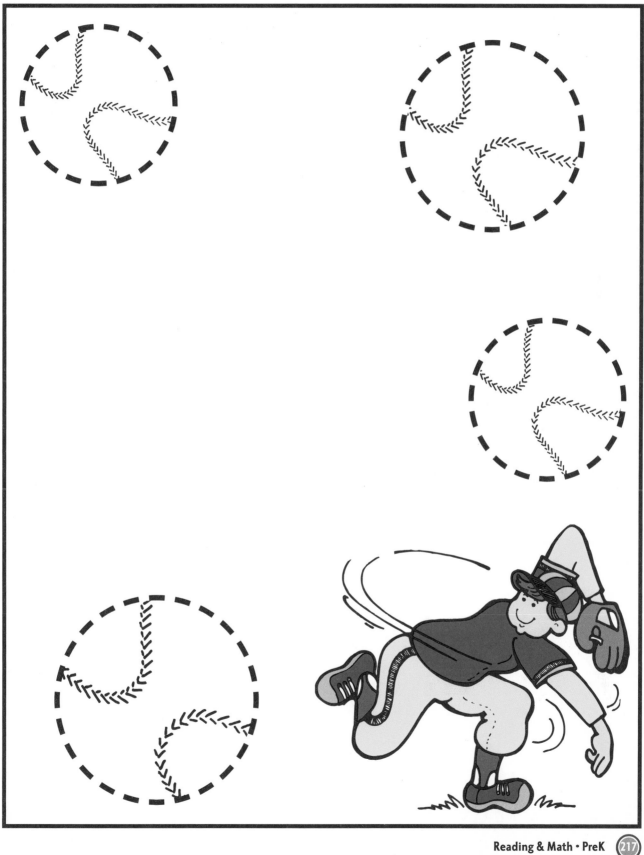

Trace and color the squares.

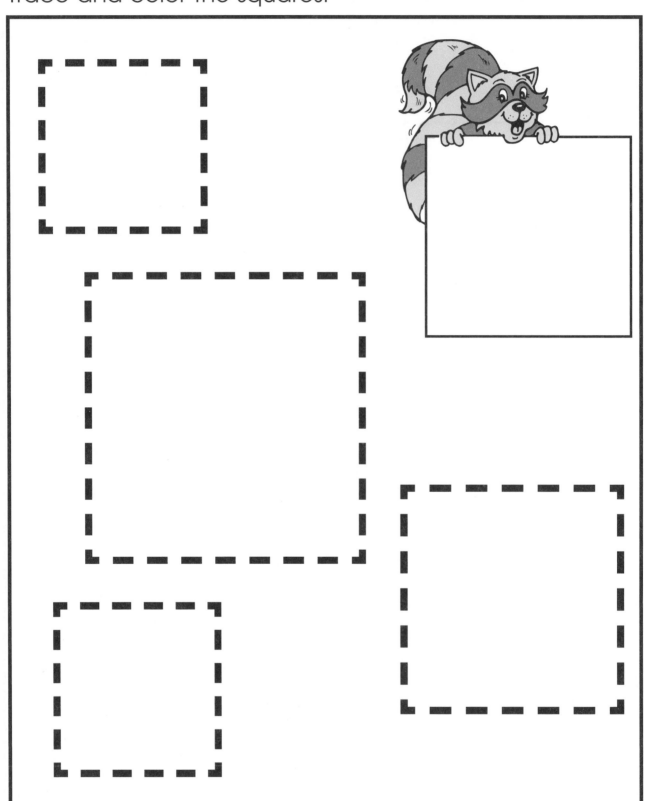

Scholastic

Color all of the squares blue.

Trace and color the ovals.

Color all of the squares blue.

Trace and color the ovals.

Scholastic

Color all of the ovals yellow.

Draw five oval eggs. Color each egg.

Scholastic

Trace and color the rectangles.

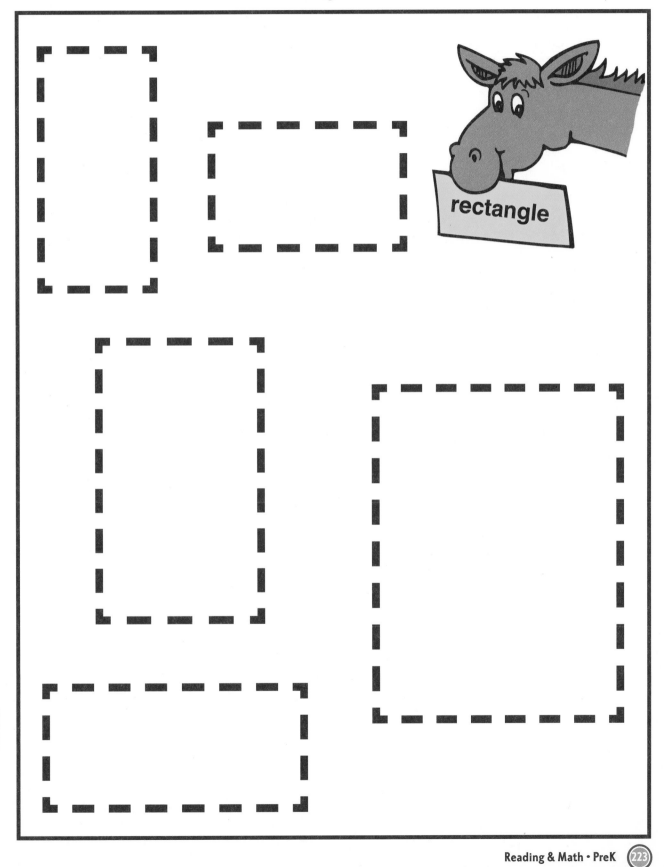

rectangle

Trace each rectangle. Draw a rectangle in each box just like the first one.

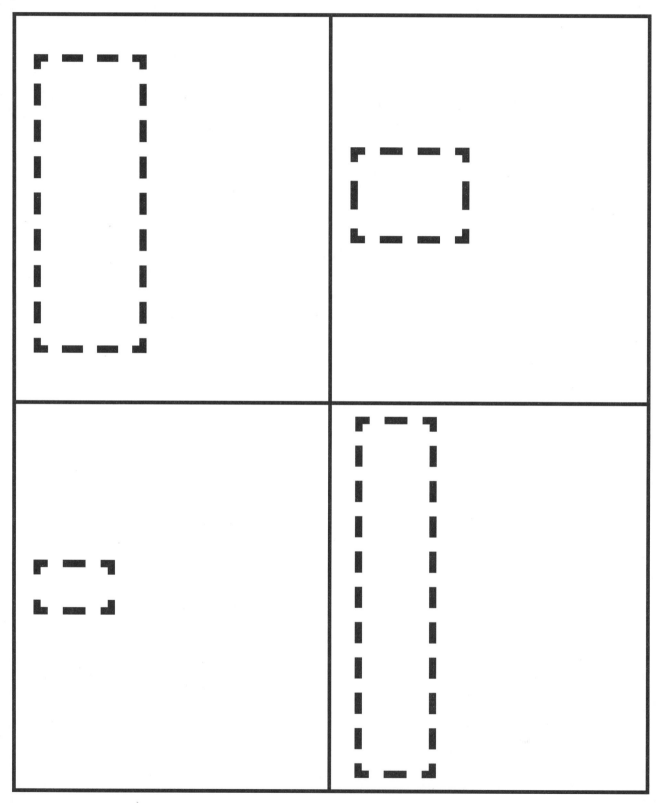

Trace and color the triangles.

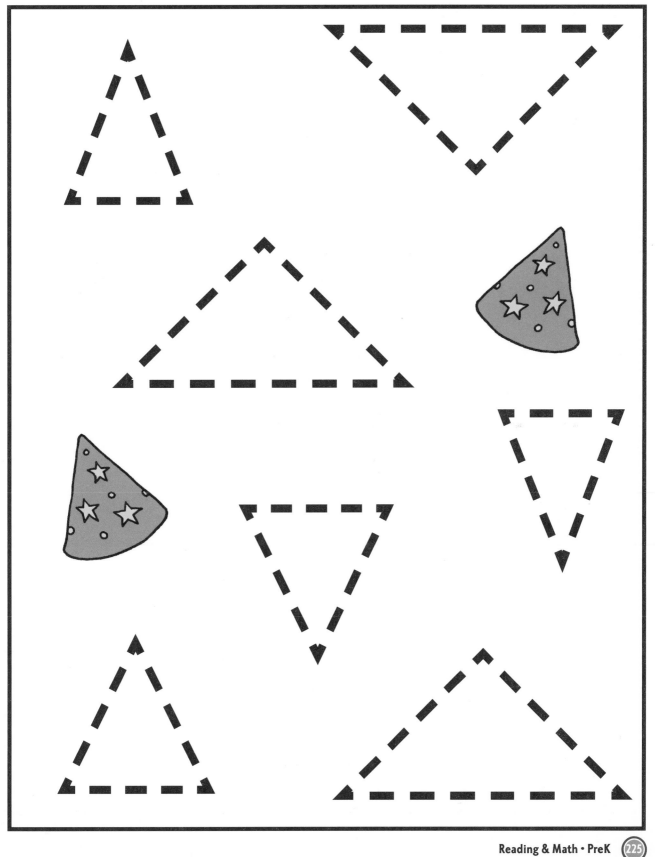

Trace the dotted line to complete the triangle wings of each butterfly.

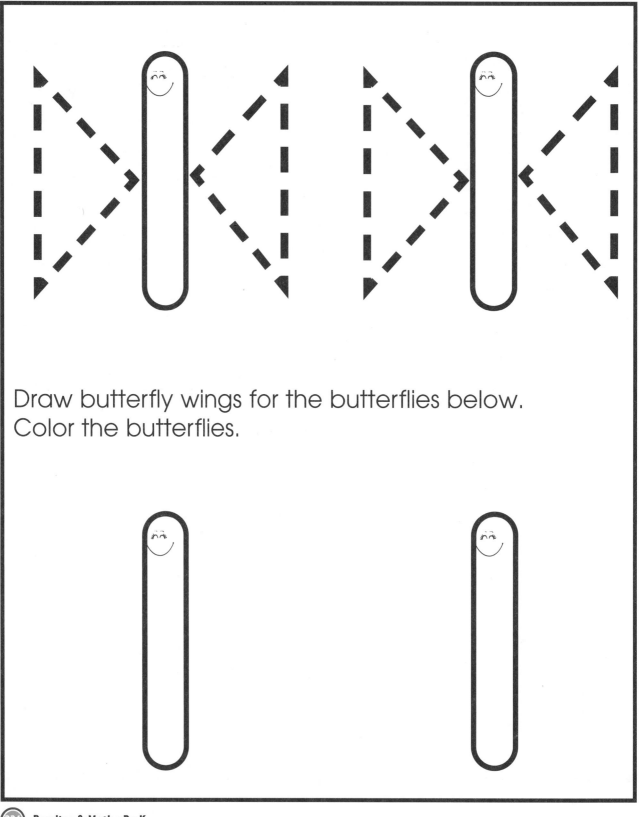

Draw butterfly wings for the butterflies below.
Color the butterflies.

Trace each triangle. Draw a triangle in each box just like the first one.

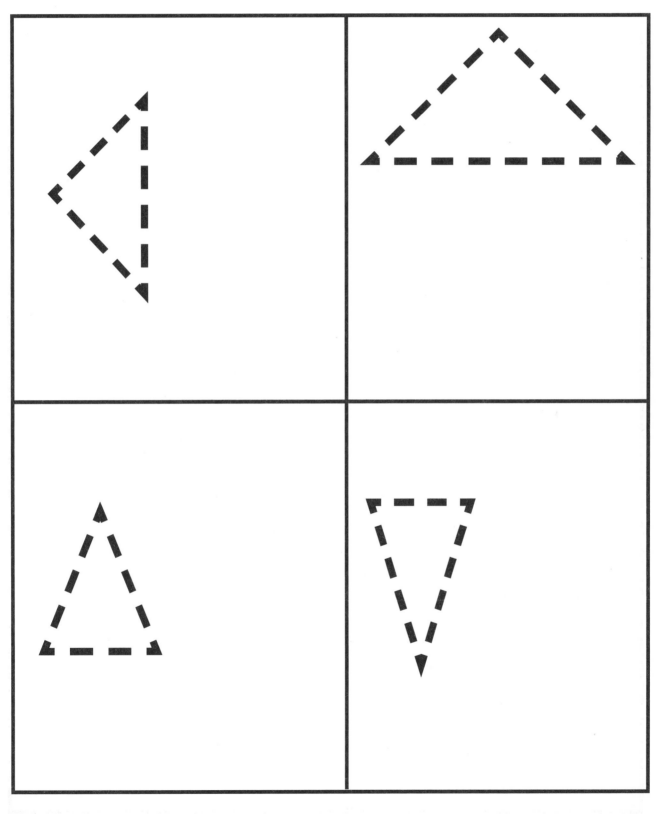

Trace and color the diamonds.

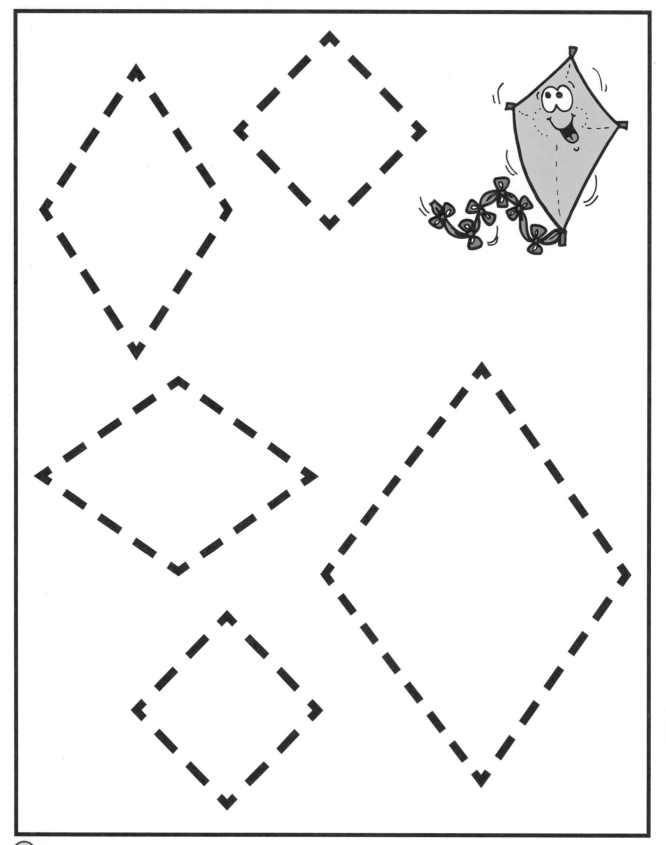

Color all of the diamonds green.

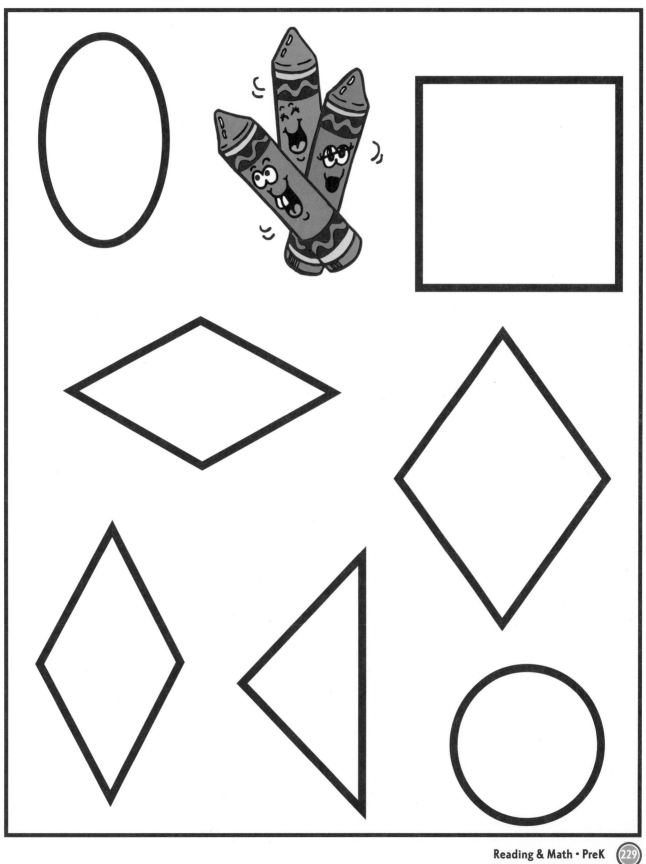

Trace the dotted lines of each diamond to complete each kite. Color the kites.

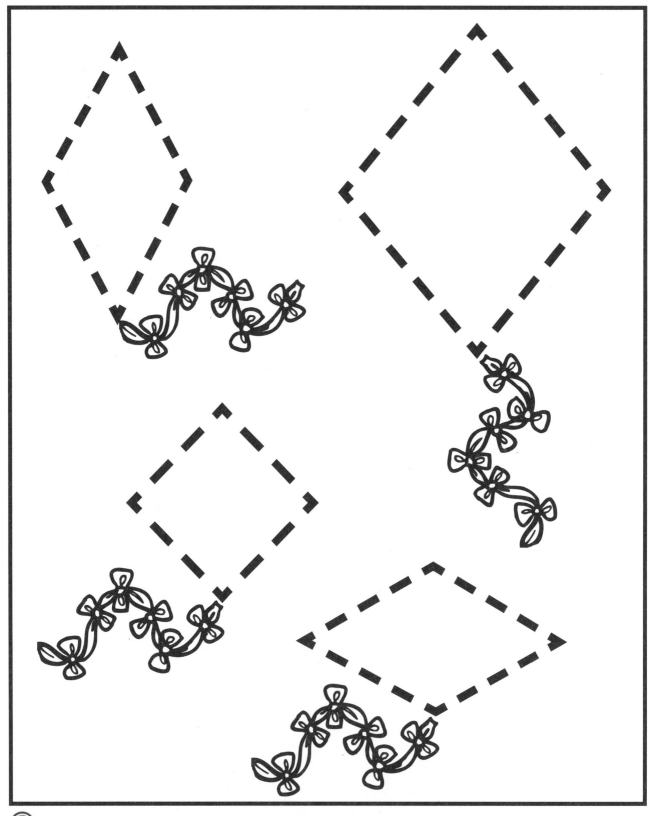

It's time to put away the blocks.

(1) Cut out the blocks.

(2) Glue each block on the shelf where it belongs.

(3) Color the blocks.

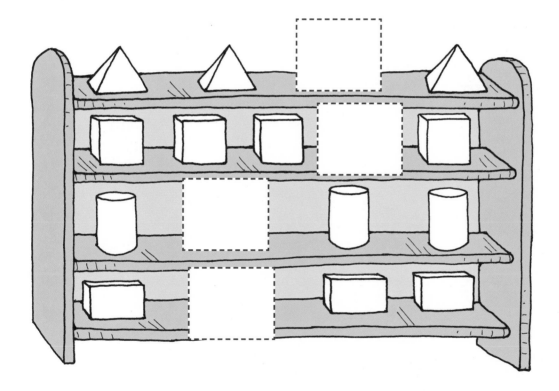

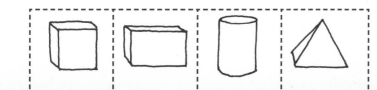

Scholastic

How many of each shape are in the snowflake?

1 **Count** the squares.

2 **Write** the number. _____

3 **Count** the triangles.

4 **Write** the number. _____

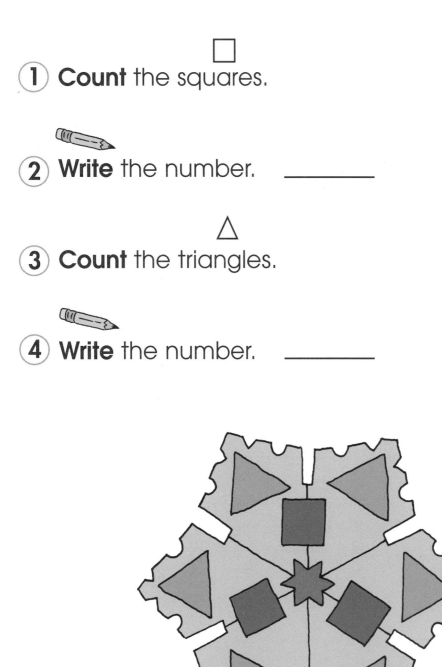

Trace and color all of the shapes. Say shape's name.

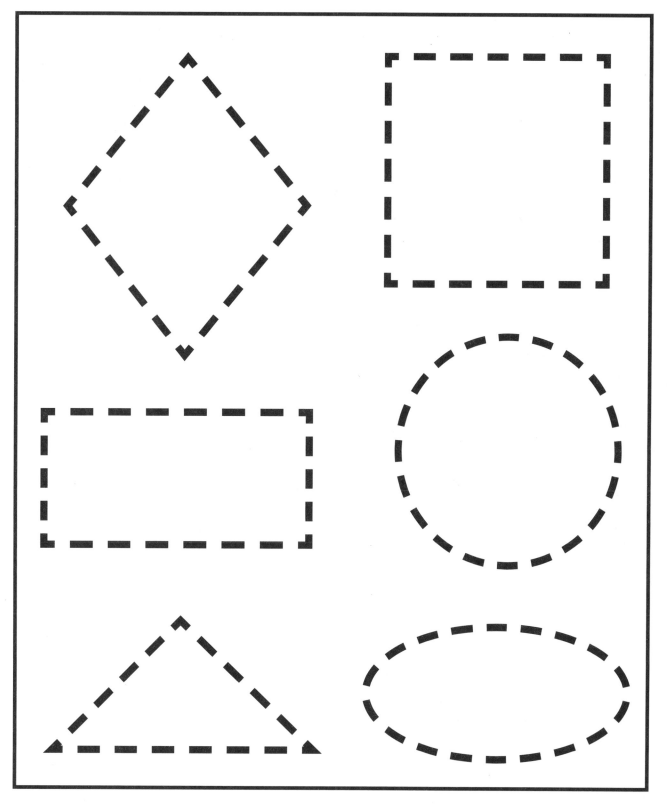

Put a circle around each circle shape.

Circle each square shape.

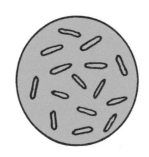

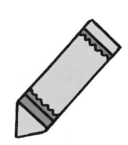

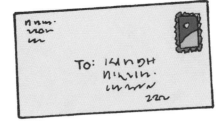

Circle each rectangle shape.

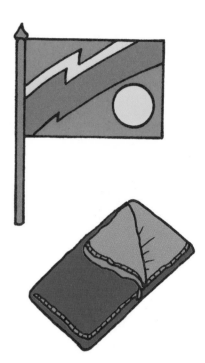

Circle each triangle shape.

Circle each diamond shape.

Circle each oval shape.

Trace each shape. Draw a line to match each object to its shape. Color.

oval

rectangle

diamond

square

Color. ◆ = black ■ = blue ▲ = red
▬ = brown ● = green ⬭ = yellow

Color each circle ◯ to show the mole's way home.

Color. ◆ = purple ▢ = yellow ▲ = orange

▭ = green ● = blue ⬭ = red

Shapes Practice Test

Read the directions to your child.

1. Fill in the bubble next to the diamond shape.

2. Fill in the bubble next to the oval shape.

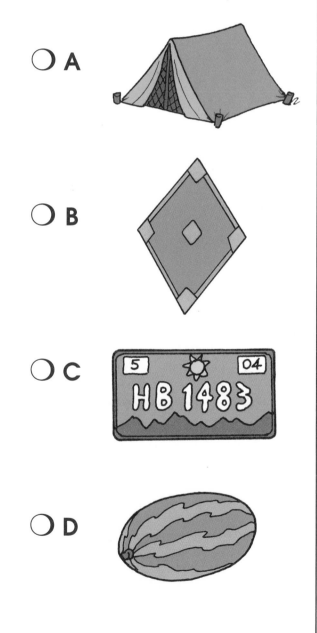

○ A

○ B

○ C

○ D

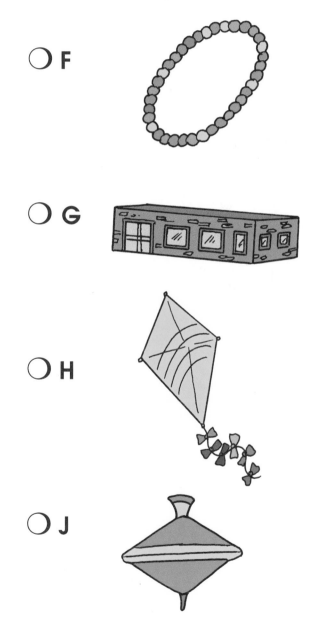

○ F

○ G

○ H

○ J

Shapes Practice Test

Read the directions to your child.

3. Fill in the bubble next to the rectangle shape.

○ **A**

○ **B**

○ **C**

○ **D**

4. Fill in the bubble next to the triangle shape.

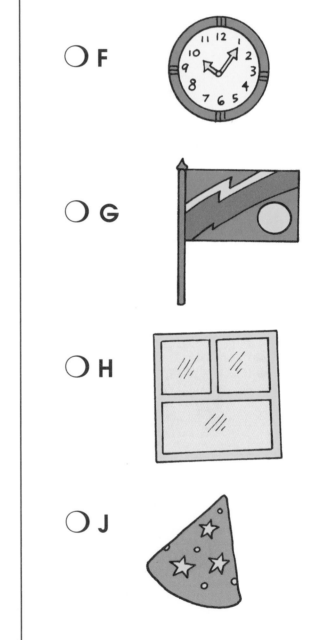

○ **F**

○ **G**

○ **H**

○ **J**

Scholastic

Shapes Practice Test

Read the directions to your child.

5. Fill in the bubble next to the circle.

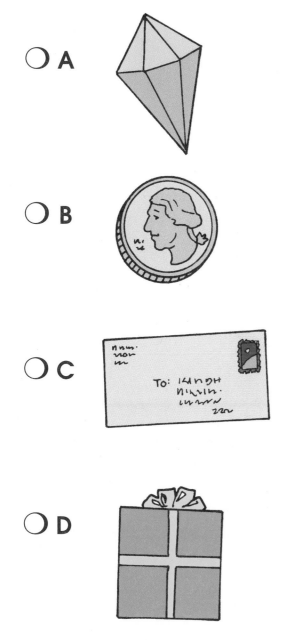

O A

O B

O C

O D

6. Fill in the bubble next to the square.

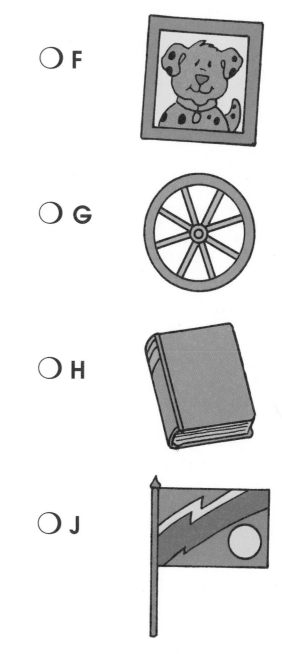

O F

O G

O H

O J

Shapes Practice Test

Read the directions to your child.

7. Count the number of circles. Fill in the bubble next to the correct number.

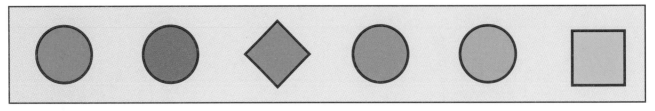

○ **A**   1

○ **B**   2

○ **C**   3

○ **D**   4

8. Count the number of triangles. Fill in the bubble next to the correct number.

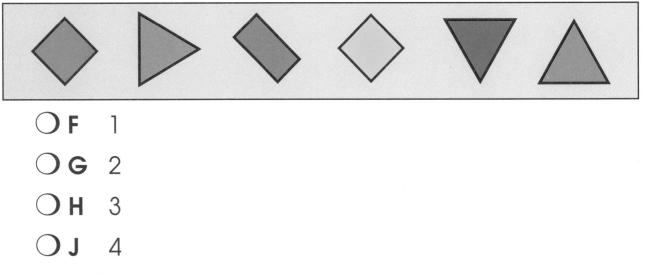

○ **F**   1

○ **G**   2

○ **H**   3

○ **J**   4

Scholastic

Patterns

Recognizing and creating patterns is a key math skill. Exploring patterns also gives kids lots of practice with visual discrimination and with colors and shapes.

What to Do

Read the directions on each page to your child. When he or she is finished, help your child check his or her work. Offer lots of praise for being such a good "pattern detective!"

Keep On Going!

Invite your child to find patterns in the world around you: stripes on a zebra at the zoo, plaid patterns on clothing, and so on.

Draw what comes next in the box at the end of each row.

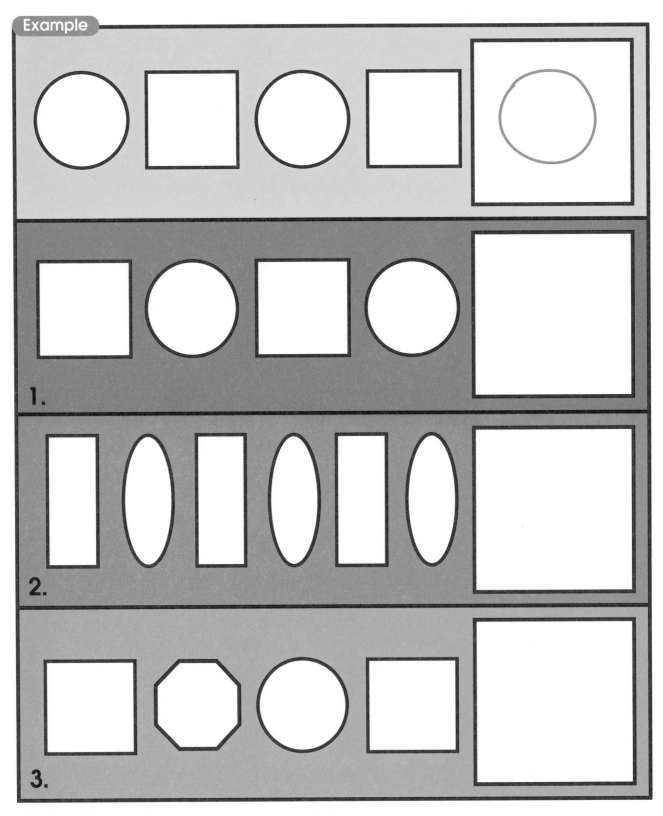

Example

Scholastic

Draw what comes next in the box at the end of each row.

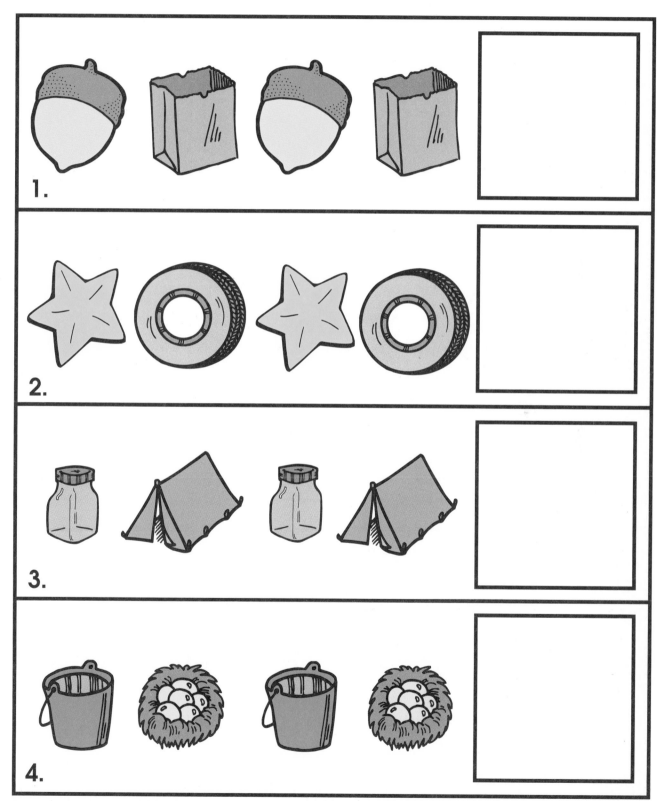

1.

2.

3.

4.

Draw a line to the shape that comes next.

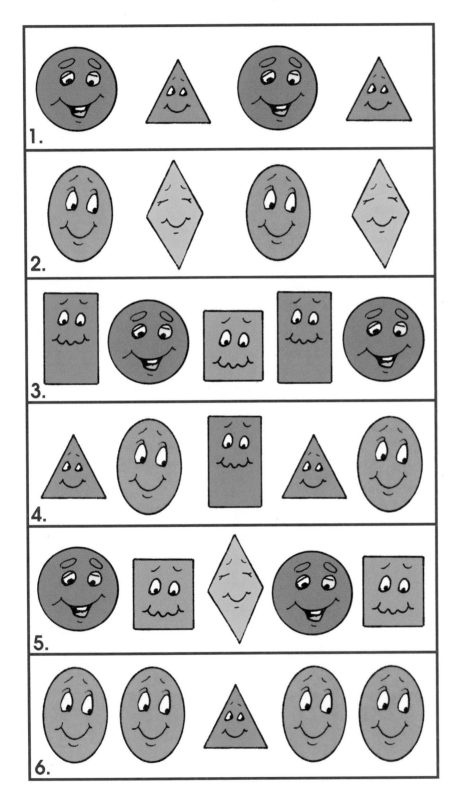

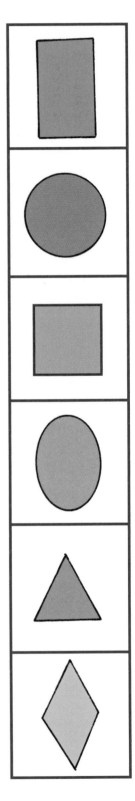

Scholastic

Circle what comes next.

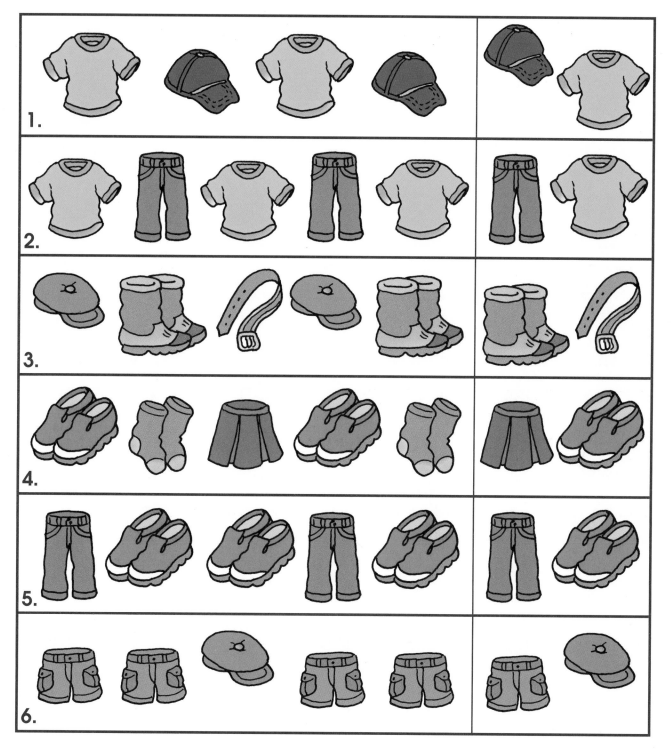

Circle what comes next.

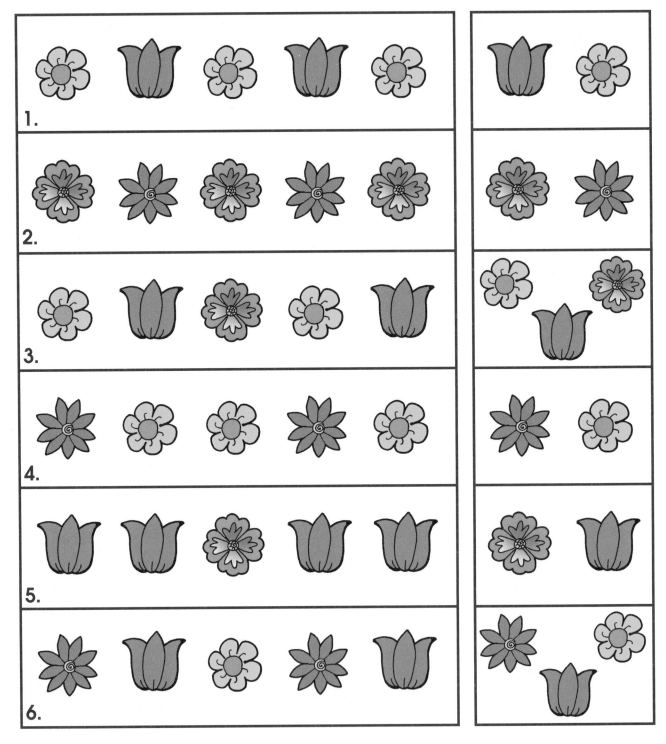

Circle what comes next.

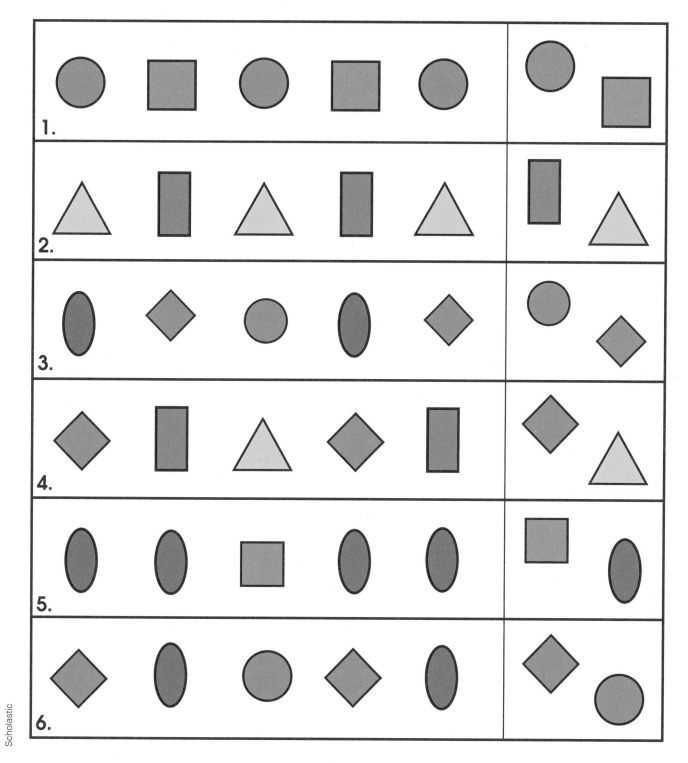

Patterns Practice Test

Read the directions to your child.

1. Fill in the bubble next to the object that comes next in the pattern.

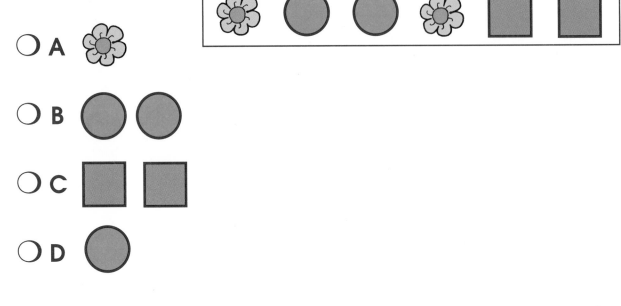

○ A 🌸

○ B ⬤ ⬤

○ C ▪ ▪

○ D ⬤

2. Fill in the bubble next to the object that comes next in the pattern.

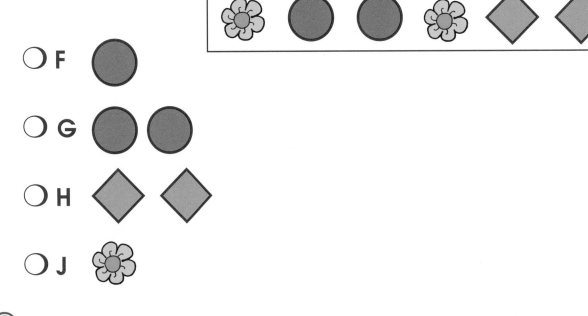

○ F ⬤

○ G ⬤ ⬤

○ H ◆ ◆

○ J 🌸

Patterns Practice Test

Read the directions to your child.

3. Fill in the bubble next to the objects that come next in the pattern.

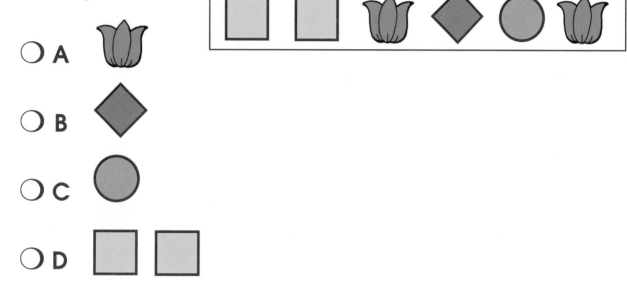

○ **A** 🌷

○ **B** ◆

○ **C** ●

○ **D** ▢ ▢

4. Fill in the bubble next to the objects that come next in the pattern.

○ **F**

○ **G**

○ **H**

○ **J**

Scholastic

Patterns Practice Test

Read the directions to your child.

5. Fill in the bubble next to the objects that come next in the pattern.

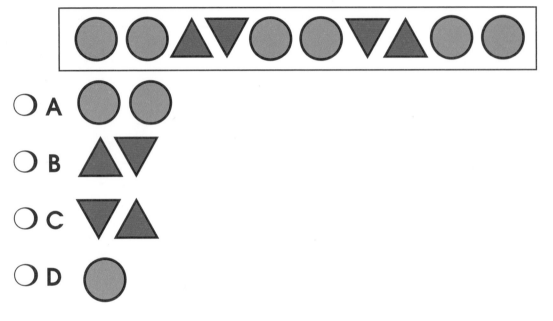

○ A

○ B

○ C

○ D

6. Fill in the bubble next to the object that comes next in the pattern.

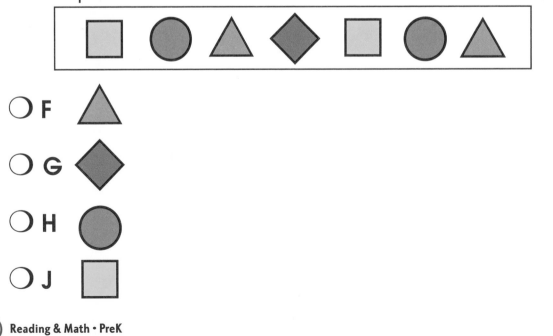

○ F

○ G

○ H

○ J

Scholastic

Patterns Practice Test

Choose a sticker to place here.

Read the directions to your child.

7. Fill in the bubble next to the object that comes next in the pattern.

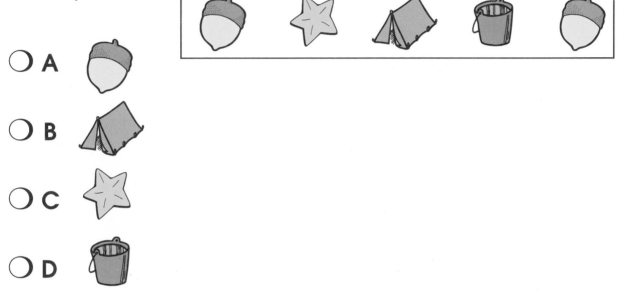

○ **A**

○ **B**

○ **C**

○ **D**

8. Fill in the bubble next to the object that comes next in the pattern.

○ **F**

○ **G**

○ **H**

○ **J**

Scholastic

Problem Solving

Problem solving is a key skill that children can apply in all school subjects and in their daily lives. In this section, children use pictures to solve problems.

What to Do

Read the directions on each page to your child. When he or she is finished, help your child check his or her work. Offer lots of praise for being such a good problem solver!

Keep On Going!

• Put together various puzzles with your child.

• Point out certain instances in which pictures can help your child understand the meaning of words they can't read yet. For instance, point out street signs with symbols that mean "Don't Walk."

Cut out the pieces of the hot dog. Paste them in the correct order to make a hot dog like the one pictured below.

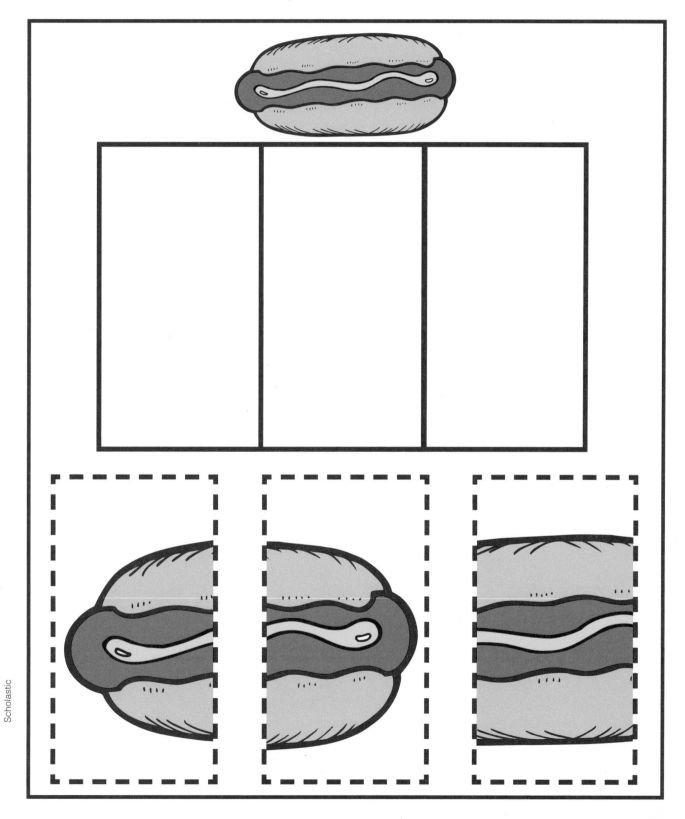

Cut out the pieces of the pencil. Paste them in the correct order to make a pencil like the one pictured below.

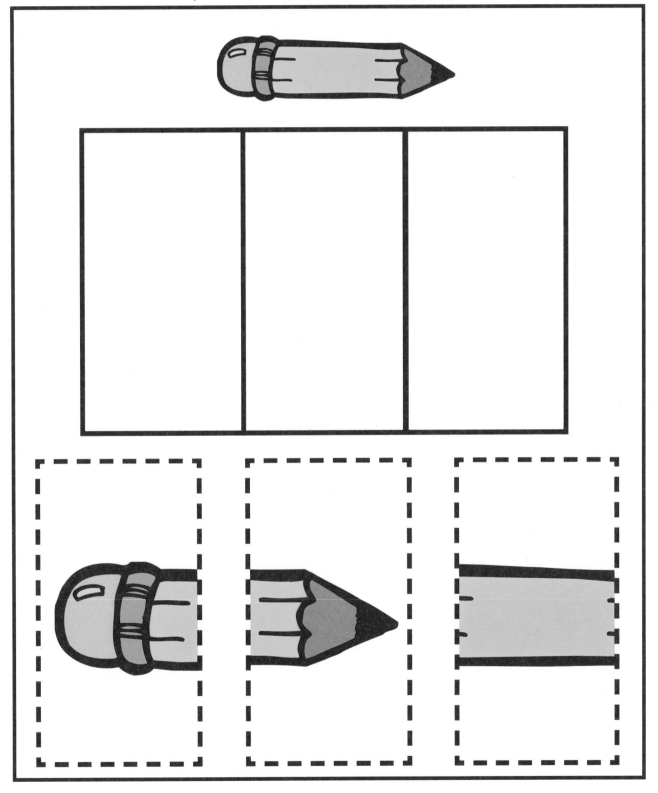

Cut out the pieces of the bone. Paste them in the correct order to make a bone like the one pictured below.

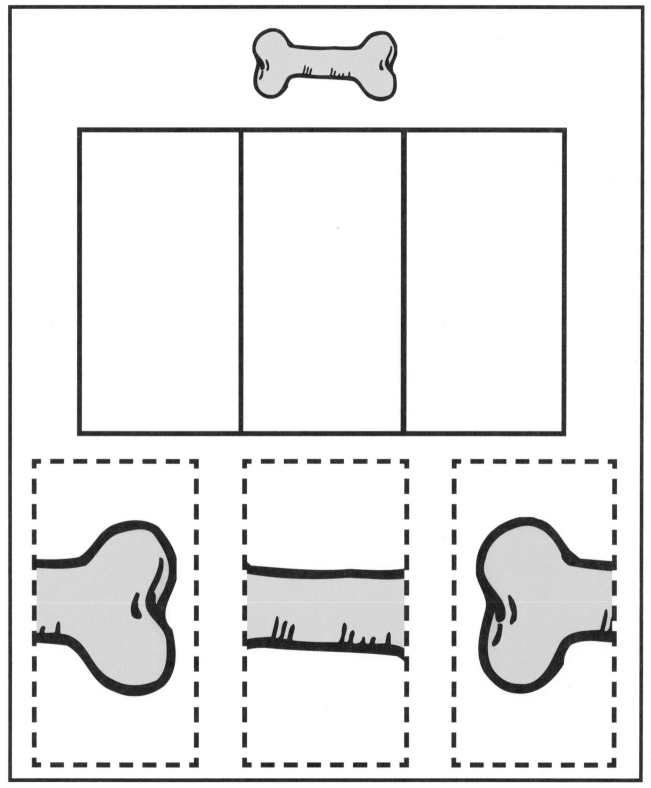

Scholastic

Cut out the pieces of the watermelon. Paste them in the correct order to make a watermelon like the one pictured below.

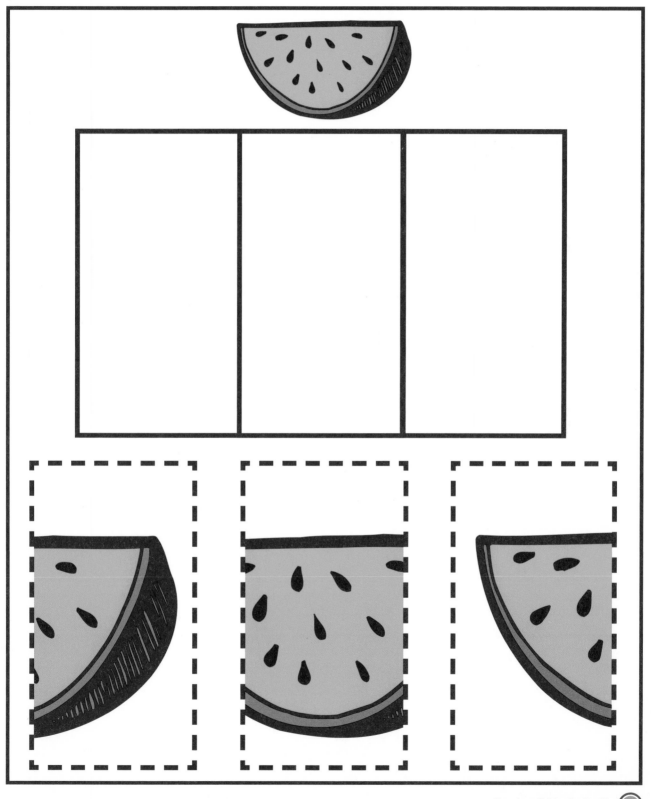

Look at the picture.

Write the number.

How many?

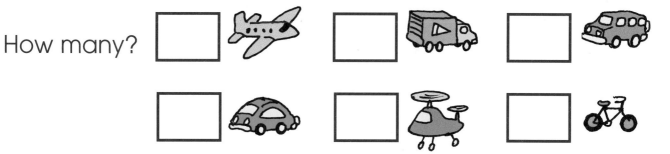

Scholastic

Circle how many you see in the picture.

🚲	1	5
🪑	4	2
🌼	8	5

🛝	6	3
🌳	7	10
🐕	2	8

🐤	9	7
🐿️	10	7
🛴	3	1

Scholastic

Look at the picture.

Write the number.

How many?

Problem Solving Practice Test

Read the directions to your child.

1. Fill in the bubble next to the number of circles in the picture.

   ○ **A** 6

   ○ **B** 7

   ○ **C** 8

   ○ **D** 9

2. Fill in the bubble next to the number of diamonds in the picture.

   ○ **F** 6

   ○ **G** 7

   ○ **H** 8

   ○ **J** 9

Scholastic

Problem Solving Practice Test

Read the directions to your child.

3. Fill in the bubble next to the number of ovals at the bottom of the picture.

○ **A** 6

○ **B** 7

○ **C** 8

○ **D** 9

5. Fill in the bubble next to the number of squares between the two tall pillars.

○ **A** 2

○ **B** 3

○ **C** 4

○ **D** 5

4. Fill in the bubble next to the number of triangles around the sun.

○ **F** 7

○ **G** 8

○ **H** 9

○ **J** 10

6. Fill in the bubble next to the number of circles between the two tall pillars.

○ **F** 1

○ **G** 2

○ **H** 3

○ **J** 4

Scholastic

Flash Cards

Cut out the word and picture flash cards on pages 271–283. Fold the cards so that the picture is on one side and the word is on the other side and tape them. Use the cards to build and reinforce new vocabulary. Add new word and picture flash cards as your child learns new words at home and in school. Also, have your child match cards with opposite meanings, such as up/down.

red

blue

orange

yellow

black

green

purple

happy

sad

apple

up	
down	
boy	
girl	
shoes	

fan

fish

bat

in

out

book

cow

dog

ball

duck

fox

moon

mitten

sock

hat

car

star

slow

fast

tree

Get Ready for
Kindergarten

Kindergarten is an exciting milestone in a child's educational life. In this section, your child will get a preview of the new skills he or she will learn in Kindergarten. The activity pages in this section were carefully chosen to help your child develop the skills necessary to be successful. Here are some of the skills and concepts covered:

- Identifying consonants and vowels

- Identifying and using consonant blends

- Understanding the relationship between letters and the sound they make

- Following directions

- Understanding words related to position

- Understanding and using special words

- Understanding the concept of words with opposite meanings

- Understanding the concepts of same and different

- Understanding basic reading-readiness skills such as sequencing and cause and effect

- Identifying, writing, and grouping numbers 1–20

- Identifying shapes such as circles, squares, rectangles, triangles, and more

- Identifying and extending patterns

- Solving problems using pictures

There are 26 letters in the alphabet. Five of the letters are vowels: *A, E, I, O,* and *U.*

All the rest are consonants.

Look at the alphabet below. Mark an **X** through the five vowels: *A, E, I, O,* and *U.* Now say the names of all the consonants.

A B C D E F G H I

J K L M N O P Q

R S T U V W X Y Z

How many consonants are there? _____

Color each balloon that has a consonant in it.

Scholastic

B *makes the sound you hear at the beginning of the words* **Bobby** *and* **bear**.

Help Bobby the bear find ten things in this store that begin with **b**. Draw a green circle around each one.

What insect buzzes around flowers and makes honey?

Scholastic

D *makes the sound you hear at the beginning of the words* **doctor** *and* **Dave**.

Look in Doctor Dave's bag. Color only the pictures that begin with **d**. Put an **X** on the pictures that do not begin with **d**.

She is another kind of doctor. She works on your teeth. Her job begins with *d*. Who is she?

Scholastic

Help Larry Last find the last sound that each word makes. Circle the correct letter under each lunchbox.

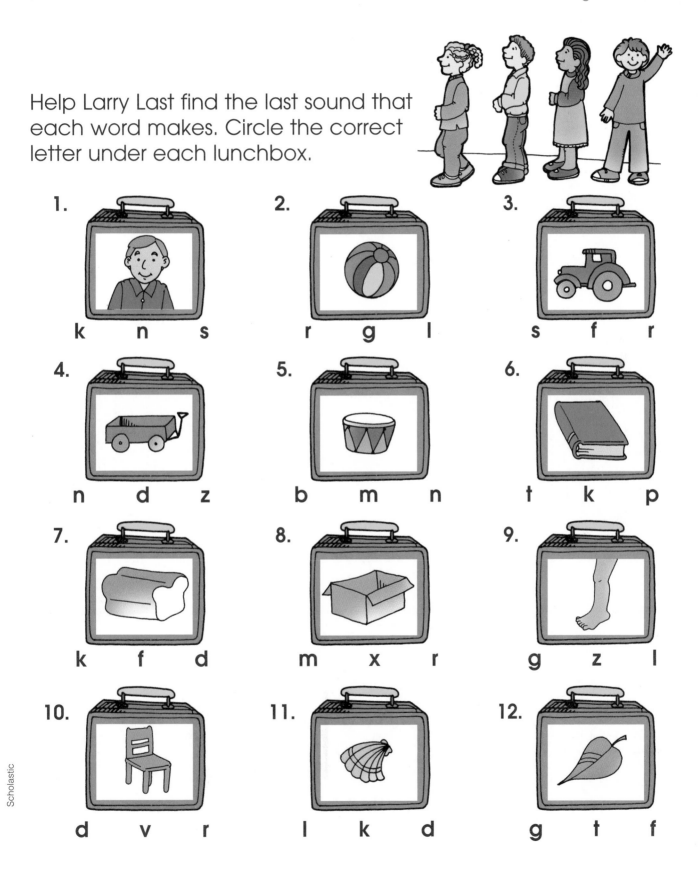

1.

k   n   s

2.

r   g   l

3.

s   f   r

4.

n   d   z

5.

b   m   n

6.

t   k   p

7.

k   f   d

8.

m   x   r

9.

g   z   l

10.

d   v   r

11.

l   k   d

12.

g   t   f

Scholastic

 There are 26 letters in the alphabet. Five of the letters are **vowels**. *They are* a, e, i, o, *and* u.

Look at the alphabet train.
> **Color the *a* car red.**
> **Color the *e* car blue.**
> **Color the *i* car orange.**
> **Color the *o* car purple.**
> **Color the *u* car green.**

 Sometimes the letter y *can be a vowel.*

> **Color the *y* car yellow.**

Look at each store sign. Circle each vowel you can find. There are 13 of them.

Scholastic

The **consonant-vowel-consonant rule:** *When only one vowel comes between consonants, that vowel is usually short.*

Unscramble the letters to spell each word. Circle the short vowel.

1. atr _rat_

2. aht _hat_

3. ktac _tack_

4. mkas _mask_

5. naf _fan_

6. plam _lamp_

7. pca _cap_

8. dDa _Dad_

9. tarp _trap_

10. dahn _hand_

11. palc _clap_

12. cklab _black_

Circle the things in the picture that rhyme with **rat** .

hat

shirt

pants

bat

trees

cat

mat

Name two things that rhyme with *rat* that are not in the picture.

Scholastic

There are 26 letters in the alphabet. The vowels are **A**, **E**, **I**, **O**, and **U**. All the rest are consonants. Color each consonant yellow.

A B C D E F G H I

J K L M N O P Q

R S T U V W X Y Z

 A **consonant blend** is when two consonants are side by side in a word, and you hear both sounds blended together. For example, you hear both the t and the r, blended together, in the word **tree**.

Draw a red circle around the two consonants that are side by side.

tree   **snow**   **fly**   **drum**

Scholastic

➡️ **Bl** *makes the sound you hear at the beginning of the words* **Blake** *and* **bluebird**.

Draw a line from each **bl** word to its matching picture. Then draw a blue circle around the letters **bl** in each word.

black

blanket

blimp

blindfold

blocks

blizzard

blouse

💡 You have this inside you. It is red. Your heart pumps it through your body. It begins with *bl*. What is it?

Scholastic

Br *makes the sound you hear at the beginning of the words* **Brady** *and* **brontosaurus**.

Brady the brontosaurus has made a puzzle for you. Use the picture clues and the Word Box to help you. Write the answers in the puzzle next to the correct number.

Word Box

brain	bride	broom	bridge
bread	brush	bricks	bracelet

Across

2.
4.
6.
8.

Down

1.
3.
5.
7.

Read the directions to your child.
Imagine that tomorrow is your birthday.

① **Color** the cake with your favorite colors.

② **Cut out** the candles.

③ How old will you be on your next birthday?

Write that number here: _____

④ **Glue** that number of candles on the cake.

Scholastic

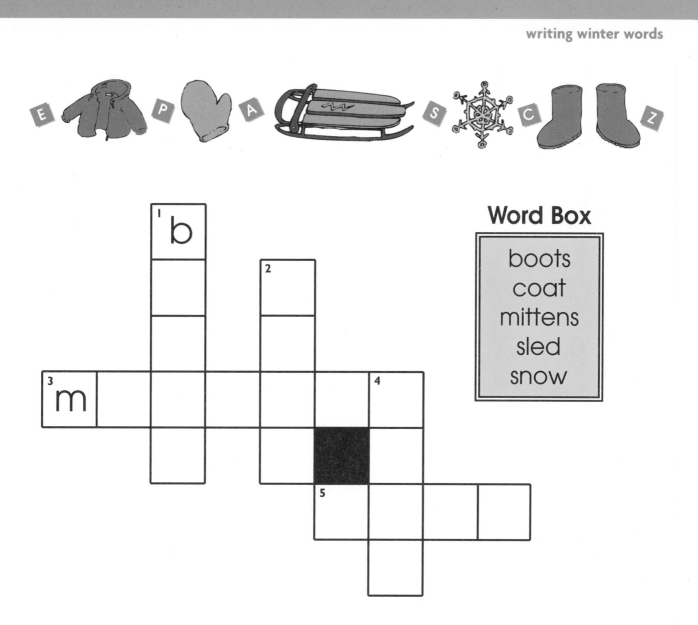

Word Box

boots
coat
mittens
sled
snow

Across

3.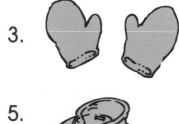

5.

Down

1.

2.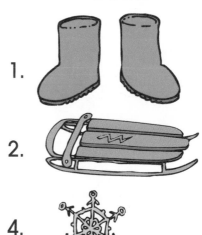

4.

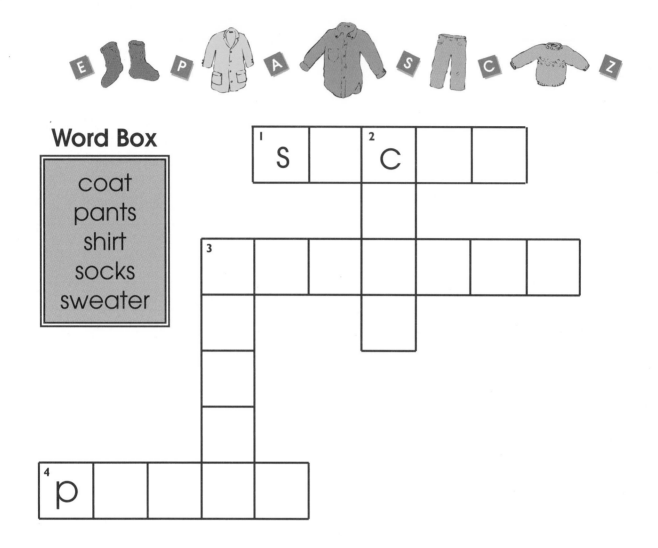

Word Box

coat
pants
shirt
socks
sweater

¹S		²C		

³						

⁴p				

Across

1.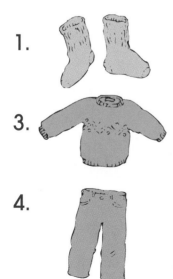

3.

4.

Down

2.

3.

Scholastic

Word Box

flower
leaves
pots
roots
seeds

f l _ _ _ r

p _ _

s _ _ _ _

Think and draw.

1. Draw a △ **ABOVE** the car.

2. Draw a △ **BELOW** the bat.

3. Draw a △ **UNDER** the snail.

4. Draw a △ **ON** the dinosaur.

5. Draw a △ **BEHIND** the class.

6. Draw a △ **AHEAD** of the cowboy.

Look at the big picture.
Which small picture came before?
Check ✔ that picture. Tell how you know.

Write the missing numbers.

Connect the dots from **1** to **10**.

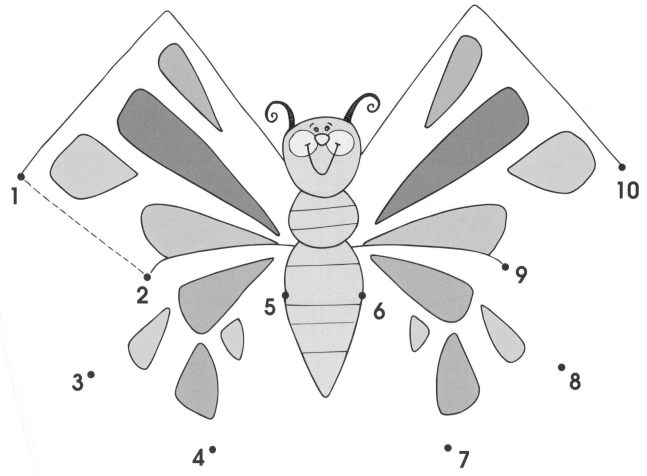

Count the spots on each picture.

Circle the correct number word.

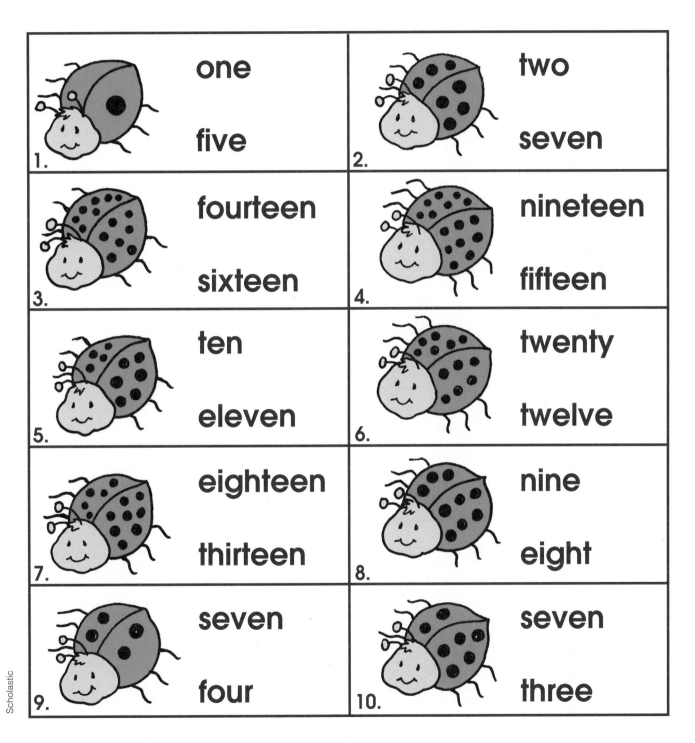

1. one
   five

2. two
   seven

3. fourteen
   sixteen

4. nineteen
   fifteen

5. ten
   eleven

6. twenty
   twelve

7. eighteen
   thirteen

8. nine
   eight

9. seven
   four

10. seven
    three

Scholastic

Draw a circle around each group of 11.

Draw a square around each group of 12.

Color.　11 = yellow　　12 = black　　13 = blue

14 = white　　15 = orange　　16 = green

17 = red　　18 = purple　　19 = brown

20 = pink

Connect the dots from **1** to **20**.

Scholastic

Count. Circle the dog with **less**.

Say the words. Color the pictures.

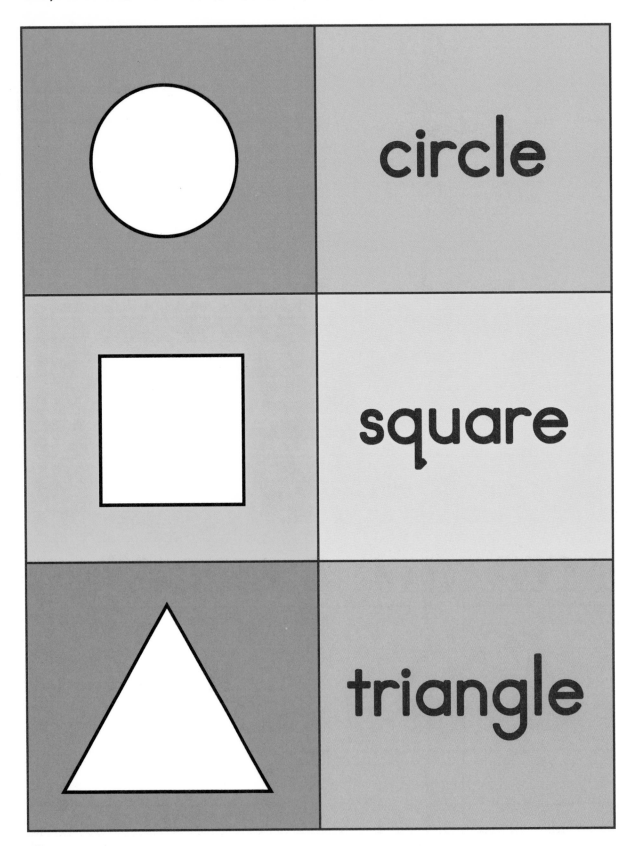

circle

square

triangle

Color the diamonds purple. Color the ovals yellow.

Draw what comes next in the box at the end of each row.

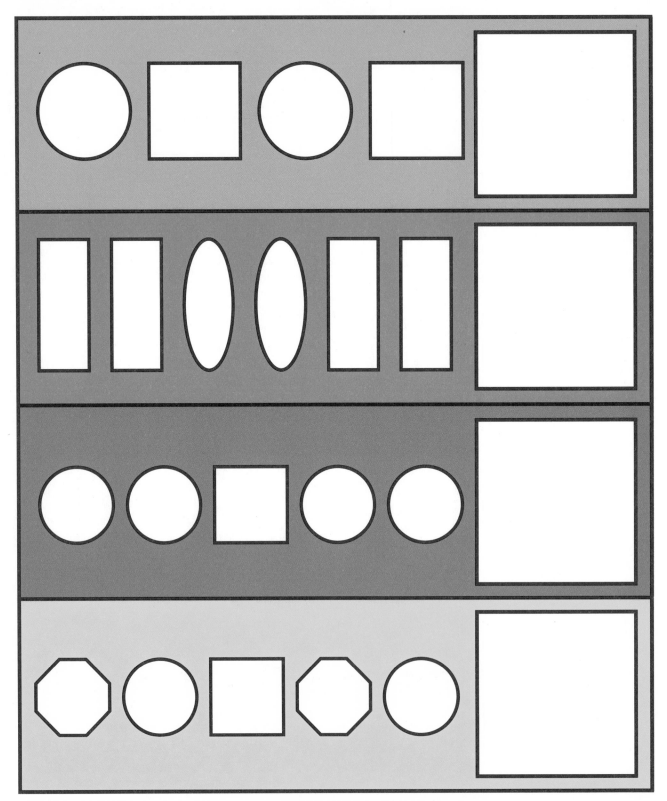

Help the sunshine reach the flowers.

Answer Key

READING/LANGUAGE ARTS

The Alphabet/Manuscript Handwriting

Page 14–29, 32–47, 50–65
Review that child has formed appropriate letters and colored pictures.

Page 30–31, 48–49, 66–67
Review that child has matched upper- and lowercase letters.

Page 68
Review that letters/dots are connected in alphabetical order to form a spaceship.

Page 69–70
1. E   2. I   3. M   4. Q

Page 71–72
1. u   2. y   3. I   4. v

Following Directions

Page 74–76
Review that directions have been followed.

Page 77
Review that each number in the picture is circled for a total of 9 numbers.

Page 78
First row: 2nd house,
Second row: 3rd house,
Third row: 1st house

Page 79
Child holding woman's hand, child with safety gear

Page 80–83
1. C   2. H   3. A   4. J
5. D   6. G   7. A   8. G

Basic Concepts

Page 85–98
Review that directions have been followed.

Page 99–102
1. C   2. G   3. A   4. G
5. A   6. G   7. C   8. F

Reading Readiness

Page 104
1. 3, 2, 1   2. 2, 1, 3

Page 105
1. 1, 2, 3   2. 1, 2, 3   3. 2, 1, 3

Page 106
1. 1, 2   2. 2, 1   3. 2, 1   4. 1, 2
5. 1, 2   6. 2, 1

Page 107
1. cow 2. doll 3. hat 4. flower
5. net 6. book 7. bone

Page 108
Review that lines are drawn between matching objects.

Page 109
1. b   2. c   3. b   4. a
5. c   6. c

Page 110
1. a, d   2. a, b   3. a, c   4. a, d

Page 111
1. a, d   2. b, d   3. a, b   4. c, d

Page 112
1. b, c   2. a, c   3. b, c   4. a, b
5. a, c

Page 113
Review that lines are drawn between matching objects.

Page 114
Review that lines are drawn between matching objects.

Page 115
1. d   2. c   3. b   4. a

Page 116
1. d   2. a   3. c   4. c
5. b

Page 117
roller skates on horse, unicorn, cat walking a dog, turtle driving, plane on street

Page 118
1. b   2. c

Page 119–122
1. A   2. H   3. C   4. H
5. D   6. G   7. D   8. H

Thinking Skills

Page 124
1. b, c, d   2. b, c, d
3. a, b, c   4. a, b, c

Page 125
1. a, b, d   2. a, c, d
3. a, b, c   4. a, b, d

Page 126
1. a, c, d   2. a, c, d
3. a, b, c   4. a, b, d
5. a, c, d

Page 127
bat/ball, web/spider, hammer/nail, saw/log

Page 128
cake/party hat, bed/pillow, ballerina/ballet shoes, hat/boots, feet/socks, toothbrush/paste

Scholastic

Page 129
1. d   2. d   3. d   4. d

Page 130
1. a   2. b   3. b   4. a
5. b   6. b

Page 131
police officer/car,
baker/bowl with spoon and cup,
construction worker/tools,
doctor/stethoscope,
firefighter/hydrant,
waitress/hamburger

Page 132
1. b   2. c   3. a

Page 133
Review that lines are drawn between
matching pictures.

Page 134
doll, bicycle, ball and mitt, teddy bear,
top

Page 135
green: c, e, g, h, j
blue: f, i
purple: a, b, d

Page 136
1. c   2. b   3. c   4. b
5. a

Page 137–140
1. C   2. F   3. C   4. J
5. C   6. J   7. B   8. G

Word Building
Page 142–155
Review that directions have been
followed.

Page 156
1. b   2. a   3. b   4. a

Page 157
1. a   2. b   3. a   4. b

Page 158
Review that directions have been
followed.

Page 159
1. over   2. under

Page 160
horse, fox, pig

Page 161
Review that directions have been
followed.

Page 162
1. a   2. b   3. a   4. a
5. a

Page 163
Review that body parts match body
names.

Page 164
1. a, c, e   2. a, d, e
3. a, b, e   4. b
5. a, e

Page 165–166
Review that directions have been
followed.

Page 167
Review your phone number.

Page 168–171
1. B   2. G   3. C   4. H
5. D   6. G   7. A   8. G

MATHEMATICS
Numbers & Number Concepts
Page 173–192
Review that numbers and words are
formed and directions followed.

Page 193
Review that directions have been
followed.

Page 194
2 horses, 3 pigs, 4 sheep, 2 cows

Page 195
Circle: 1, 6, 8   Square: 3, 5, 7

Page 196
Circle: 3, 5, 7   Square: 1, 8, 9

Page 197
Circle: 1, 3, 5   Square: 2, 7, 9

Page 198
Review that lines match numbers
with objects.

Page 199
Red: 3, 6   Yellow: 4, 8, 9

Page 200
Blue: 1, 5, 7   Green: 3, 9

Page 201
Review that correct number of
objects is circled in each row.

Page 202
Review that each section is colored
correctly.

Page 203
Review that dots are connected in the
correct order.

Page 204
Review that correct missing number is filled in.

Page 205
Review that equal groups are circled.

Page 206
Review that equal groups match.

Page 207
1. b   2. a   3. a   4. b
5. b

Page 208
Review that dog with more spots in each picture is colored.

Page 209
1. a   2. a   3. b   4. b
5. a

Page 210–3
1. D   2. H   3. A   4. J
5. D   6. G   7. B   8. H

Shapes
Page 215–230
Review that all shapes are traced, colored and drawn according to the directions.

Page 231
Review that shapes are cut and glued into appropriate rows.

Page 232
2. 3   4. 6

Page 233–240
Review that directions have been followed.

Page 241–244
1. B   2. F   3. D   4. J
5. B   6. F   7. D   8. H

Patterns
Page 246
1. square   2. rectangle
3. hexagon

Page 247
1. acorn   2. star
3. jar   4. pail

Page 248
1. circle   2. oval
3. square   4. rectangle
5. diamond   6. triangle

Page 249
1. shirt   2. pants
3. belt   4. skirt
5. shoes   6. hat

Page 250
1. pink flower   2. blue flower
3. orange flower   4. yellow flower
5. orange flower   6. yellow flower

Page 251
1. square   2. rectangle
3. circle   4. triangle
5. square   6. circle

Page 252–255
1. A   2. J   3. D   4. J
5. B   6. G   7. C   8. F

Problem Solving
Page 257–263
Review that pictures are pasted in the correct order.

Page 265
3 airplanes, 4 trucks, 5 vans,
5 cars, 2 helicopters, 1 bicycle

Page 266
1 bicycle, 4 benches, 5 flowers,
3 slides, 10 trees, 2 dogs, 9 birds,
7 squirrels, 3 scooters

Page 267
3 caterpillars, 5 flies, 4 bees,
2 butterflies, 1 ladybug,
2 grasshoppers

Page 268–269
1. D   2. H   3. C   4. J
5. D   6. J

GET READY FOR KINDERGARTEN

Page 286
21 consonants,
Color: F, M, B, J, L, X

Page 287
bird, ball, belt, boat, banana, basket, bell, books, boots, bat

Page 288
Color: dog, duck, dice, dollar, domino, deer, dinosaur, door

Page 289
1. n   2. l   3. r   4. n
5. m   6. k   7. d   8. x
9. g   10. r   11. l   12. f

Page 290
Review that directions have been followed.

Page 291
1. r<u>a</u>t 2. h<u>a</u>t 3. t<u>a</u>ck 4. m<u>a</u>sk 5. f<u>a</u>n
6. l<u>a</u>mp 7. c<u>a</u>p 8. D<u>a</u>d 9. tr<u>a</u>p
10. h<u>a</u>nd   11. cl<u>a</u>p   12. bl<u>a</u>ck

Page 292
hat, cat, mat, bat

Page 293
ten, hen, pen, men

Page 294
1. gate, late, skate
2. fail, pail, tail
3. save, wave, brave
4. gain, stain, train

Page 295
Circle: tr, sn, fl, dr

Page 296
Review that words and pictures match.

Page 297
1. bread   2. brain
3. bracelet   4. bride
5. brick   6. bridge
7. broom   8. brush

Page 298
Review that directions have been followed.

Page 299
1. boots   2. sled
3. mittens   4. snow
5. coat

Page 300
1. socks   2. coat
3. sweater   3. shirt
4. pants

Page 301

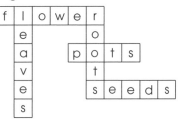

Page 302
Review that directions have been followed.

Page 303
1, 3, 2—Review writing.

Page 304
1. b   2. a   3. c

Page 305
Check on bread/peanut butter.
Review writing.

Page 306
Review that directions have been followed.

Page 307
1. one   2. seven
3. fourteen   4. fifteen
5. ten   6. twelve
7. thirteen   8. nine
9. four   10. seven

Page 308–310
Review counting and that directions have been followed.

Page 311
1. b   2. a   3. a   4. b
5. a

Page 312–313
Review that directions have been followed.

Page 314
1. circle   2. oval, oval
3. square   4. square

Page 315
Review that directions have been followed.

Scholastic

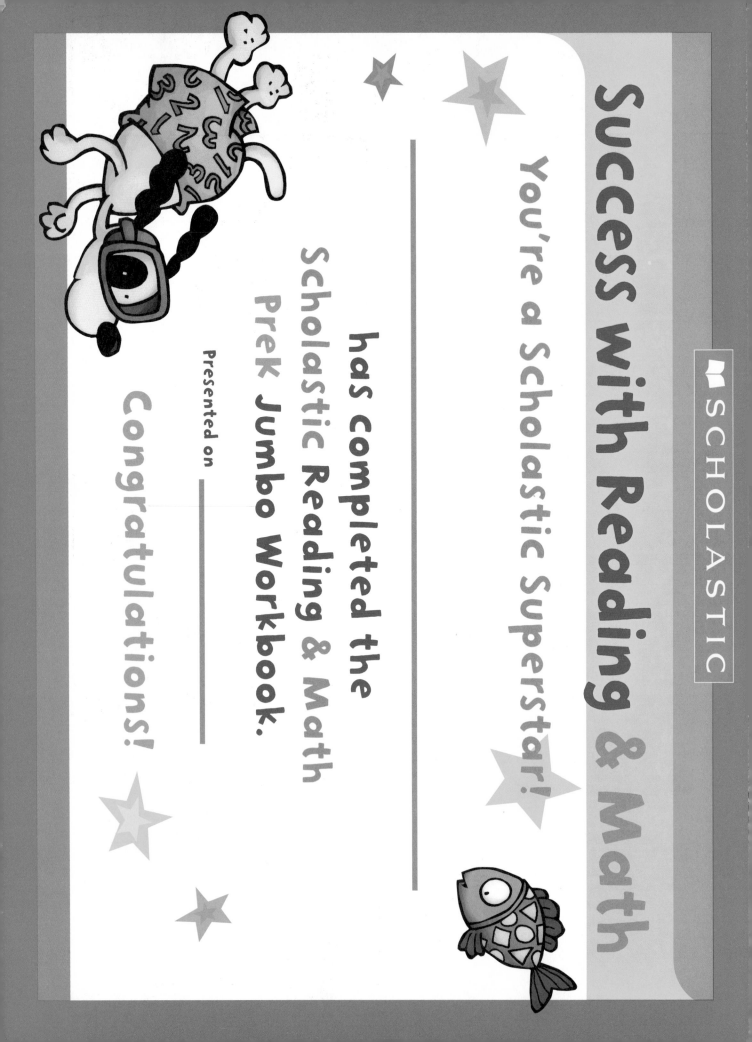

SCHOLASTIC

Success with Reading & Math

You're a Scholastic Superstar!

_____

has completed the
Scholastic Reading & Math
Prek Jumbo Workbook.

Presented on

_____

Congratulations!

894173 PO #523282